Keeping Our EarTh Green

ISBN-13: 978-0-8249-6825-0 (softcover)
ISBN-13: 978-0-8249-6824-3 (hardcover)

Published by Williamson Books
An imprint of Ideals Publications
A Guideposts Company
Nashville, Tennessee
www.idealsbooks.com

Library of Congress Cataloging-in-Publication Data

Castaldo, Nancy F. (Nancy Fusco), 1962-
  Keeping our earth green / by Nancy F. Castaldo, Jim Caputo.
     p. cm. -- (Kids can!)
  Includes index.
  ISBN 978-0-8249-6825-0 (softcover : alk. paper) -- ISBN 978-0-8249-6824-3
(hardcover : alk. paper)
  1. Green movement--Juvenile literature. 2. Conservation of natural
resources--Juvenile literature. I. Caputo, Jim. II. Title.
  GE195.5.C37 2008
  363.7--dc22
                         2008009423

Project Editor: Patricia Pingry
Designed by Jenny Hancock

Printed and bound in China

10 9 8 7 6 5 4 3 2 1

Photographs: p. 11 Donora smog: Copyright, Pittsburgh Post-Gazette, 2008, all rights reserved. Reprinted
with permission; p. 17 Photo courtesy NASA Goddard Space Flight Center; p. 34 Cuyahoga River Fire,
Special Collections, Cleveland State University Library, used by permission; p. 44 Photo courtesy of the
Exxon Valdez Oil Spill Trustee Council; p. 47 Photo courtesy NASA; p. 58 and 59, National Oceanic and
Atmospheric Administration/Department of Commerce; p. 64 courtesy Environmental Protection Agency;
p. 78 Bald Eagle, United States Bureau of Reclamation, Department of the Interior; p. 108 Three Mile Island
nuclear plant, NRC File Photo.

This book is dedicated to you, the reader, for choosing to make a difference and living in celebration of our Earth.

Acknowledgments

It is with my unending gratitude that I thank all those who went before who have inspired my green spirit: John
Burroughs, John Muir, Rachel Carson, Hal Borland, and Henry David Thoreau, and those still here inspiring me—
the folks at Five Rivers Environmental Center, The Sierra Club National Education Committee, and the New York
State Outdoor Education Association. Thanks to Pat Pingry, who asked me to write this book at just the right time
and the team at Williamson/Ideals; my agent, Sara; and my writing buddies Coleen Paratore, Debbi Michiko
Florence, Rose Kent, Lois Feister-Huey, Kyra Teis, Eric Luper, Liza Frennette, and Helen Mesick for their constant
support and listening ears.
        I could not have written this book without the love of my family—those who have walked with me in
the forests, helped me to hear the birds, and given me the ocean at my feet.

Keeping Our EarTh Green

Over 100 Hands-On Ways to Help Save the Earth

By Nancy F. Castaldo

Illustrations by Jim Caputo

WITHDRAWN

williamsonbooks™

Nashville, Tennessee

A Note from the Author

"People start pollution. People can stop pollution." Those words were the tagline at the end of the *Keep America Beautiful* television commercial that aired for the first time on Earth Day 1971. The commercial featured the Native American actor Chief Iron Eyes Cody who, throughout the commercial, stressed that each person has a responsibility to keep the earth clean and each person has the ability to make a difference. By the end of the *Keep America Beautiful* advertising campaign, litter had been reduced in our country by 80 percent.

That campaign occurred more than 35 years ago, but the effort to increase concern for our planet is as important as ever—some would say even more so. While the issues of keeping our air, land, and water clean are still crucial, today we also face other issues that appear daunting, such as climate change. Even so, the message remains the same: *"People start pollution. People can stop pollution."*

—NC

CONTENTS

"Live in the sunshine, swim in the sea, drink the wild air . . ."
—Ralph Waldo Emerson

Who Cares about Clean Air?

Take a deep breath. According to the Environmental Protection Agency (EPA), we breathe about 3,000 gallons of air each day. Our bodies might be able to live a week or two without food and maybe three, or even four, days without water; but we cannot live more than a few minutes without air. It is number one on our survival list, and the cleaner the better.

Clean air cannot be more important to us. Pollution of the air not only harms us, but it also damages animals, crops, trees, and even buildings and monuments. What is in the air we breathe? Not all pollution looks smoky or dirty, although smog is certainly pollution. Most pollution is not even noticeable,

including acid rain, and some pollutants are in the form of natural particles. Read on and learn what you can do to help keep our air clean.

DICTIONARY So What's Air Pollution?

The World Health Organization (WHO) has estimated that, throughout the world, air pollution will cause approximately two million premature deaths each year. The country that leads the list with the most premature deaths from air pollution is China. Each year approximately 656,000 deaths in China are attributed to indoor and outdoor air pollution.

There are several types of air pollution. One type of air pollution comes from the release of small particles into the air from burning fuel for energy. This pollution comes from automobiles, homes, industries, and perhaps even from fireplaces and barbecues.

Another type of air pollution comes from noxious gases released into the air. These gases include sulfur dioxide, carbon monoxide, nitrogen oxides, and chemical vapors. Once in the atmosphere, these chemicals form smog and acid rain.

There is also air pollution inside our homes, offices, and schools. Some of these pollutants are created by smoking and cooking.

BE GREEN PLEASE!

The Issue:
Secondhand Smoke

Scientists have determined that secondhand smoke, the smoke that we breathe in from tobacco smoke from others, is dangerous to humans. Tobacco smoke contains more than 4,000 chemicals, 200 of which are known poisons. The EPA has classified smoke pollution as a carcinogen. Smoking is banned in all federal buildings, hospitals, government buildings, museums, schools, domestic airlines, and theaters. There is no federal government smoking control legislation, so states have set up their own regulations. More and more states are banning smoking in public places, such as restaurants and workplaces.

GREEN NEWS

More and more states are passing no smoking laws. Find out what the smoking laws are in your state at http://www.smokefreeworld.com. Support smoking bans and other clean air laws that help keep the air around you pure.

DICTIONARY

So What's Secondhand Smoke?

Secondhand smoke is the smoke that is released from a cigarette or cigar that someone near you is smoking.

So What's a Carcinogen?

A *carcinogen* is a substance from the environment that can cause cancer in humans.

Reality Check

Join a group of New York teens who are exposing tobacco companies that promote their products in movies. Reality Check believes that some companies are deliberately focusing on America's youth and children in an attempt to create tomorrow's tobacco consumers. Reality Check claims that advertisements are placed at events geared to teens, in magazines geared to young readers, and at convenience stores teens frequent. And even though in 1998, the government made it illegal to place tobacco products in movies, some characters in many of today's movies are smoking or holding a cigarette. And these smokers are not confined to movies for adults. According to Reality Check, 75 percent of PG-13 rated movies and 40 percent of movies rated G and PG contain tobacco images.

Teens are shaking it up all over the country and making a difference. Find out more about New York's Reality Check at http://www.realitycheckny.org and other teen organizations in the Resources section of this book.

Try This!

The tiny hairs in your nose trap many of the particles you inhale and prevent them from entering your lungs. Use a cotton swab to clean your nose and wipe the mucus on a glass slide. Place the slide under a microscope and take a look at some of those particles. Your nose does a great filter job, doesn't it?

BE GREEN PLEASE!

The Air We Breathe

What You Need

- **Several index cards**
- **Scissors**
- **Double-sided clear tape**
- **Hole punch**
- **String**
- **Microscope or magnifying glass**

1 Cut a square out of the center of each index card, leaving a square window. Fill the window with strips of double-sided tape.

2 Punch a hole in the middle of the short side of the card, and tie a piece of string through it. Hang each card in a different spot. Hang one card near a window, another near a heat vent, another someplace outside. Leave the cards alone for a few days to collect particles from the air.

3 Take your cards down and examine them under a magnifying glass or microscope. What do you think you collected? You might find pollen, dust particles, mold, even flakes of skin from your pets or family. Some of these particles may affect your breathing and create allergic reactions or asthma. Some particles are too tiny for you to see.

4 Make a list of the ways that you can reduce the amount of particles you breathe each day.

IT Happened in The Past: Donora Smog

On Halloween night 1948, horror visited the U.S. Steel company town of Donora, Pennsylvania, when a temperature inversion descended on the town. Fumes from the smelting plants belonging to U.S. Steel blanketed the town for four days and crept into homes. The next day, twenty people were dead from the pollution, and about one-third of the town's 14,000 residents were ill. Hundreds of people were evacuated or hospitalized. The 1948 Donora incident led to the creation of the Air Pollution Control Act of 1955. This was the first federal attempt to control air pollution.

Donora, Pennsylvania, at noon on October 29, 1948

 **DICTIONARY** So What's Temperature Inversion?

Usually, air at higher altitudes is cooler because the sun warms the earth's air which then rises, where it expands and cools. Sometimes, however, the temperature of air increases as it rises. When warm air is on top of cooler air in the atmosphere, this situation is referred to as a *temperature inversion*. The warm air at the top of the atmosphere acts as a lid and traps pollutants below.

Acid Rain

Not all rain or snow that falls from the sky is as clean as your drinking water. Sometimes it is acid rain. When toxins find their way into the air, they then fall to earth when it rains or snows.

Scientists know acid rain has a lower pH than pure rain. Water generally has a neutral pH of seven, but acid rain may have a pH closer to four, meaning it is more acidic.

The sulfuric and nitric acids might come from natural sources, like volcanoes and decaying matter. More often, however, the acids come from man-made emissions of nitrogen oxide and sulfur dioxide which are byproducts of fossil fuels burned at power plants.

Winds blow the chemicals and they combine with water molecules in the atmosphere to form toxic acids. Ultimately these acids fall miles away from the plant, sometimes even in the next state or country. The acids fall in the form of rain, snow, sleet, hail, and even dew and fog. This type of pollution not only makes it difficult for people to breathe, but it can kill trees and crops and poison lakes, ponds, and streams. Acid rain can even damage the paint on an automobile.

DICTIONARY

So What's Acid Rain?

Acid rain can be rain, snow, hail, dew, or fog that has been made acidic by acids released into the air by the burning of fossil fuels.

....

So What's a pH?

The term *pH* is used to express the acidity or alkalinity of a substance where pH7 is neutral, lower numbers are more acidic, and higher numbers are more alkaline.

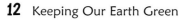

Check Your Plants

What You Need
- **2 houseplants**
- **Water**
- **Vinegar**
- **Measuring cup**

1 Place both plants in the same sunny window.

2 Water one plant with regular water.

3 Water the second plant with a mixture of half water and half vinegar which is acidic.

4 Water the plants the same way for a month.

5 Do you notice any difference? Imagine a whole forest of plants being watered with acid rain.

Check Your Home

Test your own rainwater to see if any acid rain is falling in your area.

What You Need
- **2 clean jars**
- **pH indicator strips**
- **Paper and pencil**

1 Place one jar outside during the next rainfall or snowfall.

2 After the rain or snow has stopped, bring the jar inside.

3 Place the pH strip into the liquid. Look at the indicator colors. Write down the pH of your rain.

4 Fill a second jar with tap water. Use a new test strip to test its pH and note it on your paper.

5 Is the pH of both waters about the same or does one have a much lower pH?

6 If your rain is acidic, try to find out where the acid is coming from. Where is the power plant closest to your house?

Ozone

Halting air pollution is important to our survival, not only for the oxygen we need to breathe but for another reason as well. One of the materials in our atmosphere is called *ozone*, a gas that is both helpful and dangerous, depending upon where in our atmosphere it appears.

In the stratosphere layer of the atmosphere, a layer of ozone from six to 30 miles (9.6–48 km) deep protects us from the sun's ultraviolet (UV) radiation. Medical scientists believe that increased exposure to UV radiation can cause skin cancers and cataracts to humans. The ozone layer of our atmosphere is the "good" ozone.

When ozone builds up close to earth, however, it is called a pollutant because it causes harm. Ozone occurs naturally in the air around us, and sometimes you can even smell it after or during a lightning storm. In fact, ozone can be found in smog, that nasty stuff that hangs around the air near our cities. It is dangerous to breathe, because it attacks the lungs and mucus tissues and is particularly damaging to asthmatics and the elderly.

DICTIONARY

So What's Smog?

Smog is a mixture of many chemicals that react or combine in the presence of heat and sunlight to form an atmospheric layer of hazy, brown air.

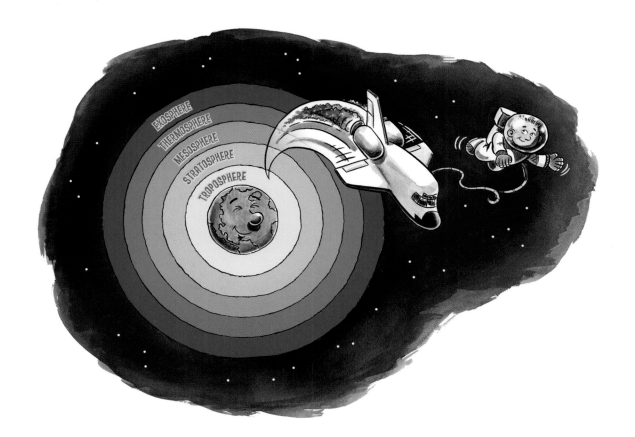

The Atmosphere

Our atmosphere is divided into four layers and the first begins right at the top of your big toe. This first layer is called the *troposphere* and is filled with the air we breathe. This is where there are clouds and our weather happens.

The next layer is the *stratosphere*. This layer begins at the top of the troposphere and extends upward for about fifty miles (80.5 km).

There is virtually no weather in this layer and is the perfect place for planes to fly.

The *mesosphere* is next and then the *thermosphere*. The thermosphere is the part of the atmosphere where there are *auroras* or northern lights.

The last layer of our atmosphere is called the *exosphere*. This is where our atmosphere merges with space.

The Issue:
Ozone Depletion

There is a thinning patch of ozone in the stratosphere 10 miles (16 km) above the South Pole. This area is so thin that the layer appears as a hole in photos taken from space. The "hole" is larger than all of North America and changes size due to the seasonal temperature changes as well as the level of pollutants which deplete the ozone. Some people confuse the ozone hole with global warming, but the depletion of ozone has nothing to do with global warming. It is caused by chemical reactions in the stratosphere.

Ozone depletion occurs from natural phenomenon. When the temperature at the South Pole falls below -126°F (-880°C), acid-bearing clouds are formed which can destroy some of the ozone. Although this natural weather phenomenon has occurred every year for eons and destroys some of the ozone, a far greater villain rises to the stratosphere from homes right here on Earth.

The largest ozone-eating pollutants are known as *chlorofluorocarbons* (CFCs), found in hair sprays, refrigerants, pesticides, and plastics. When these CFCs work their way into the stratosphere, they unleash their chlorine atoms that begin a chemical chain reaction that breaks down the ozone. One chlorine atom can destroy more than 100,000 ozone molecules, and the chlorine can remain in the atmosphere for 50 years.

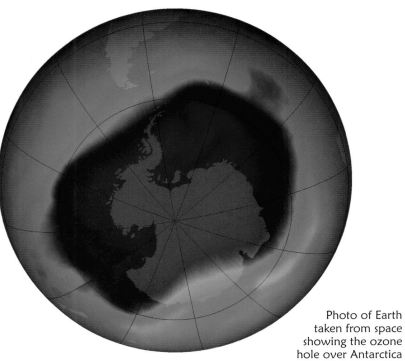

Photo of Earth taken from space showing the ozone hole over Antarctica

DICTIONARY

So What's Ozone?

Ozone is a toxic gas with a pungent odor that differs from normal oxygen (O_2) in that ozone is made up of three oxygen molecules (O_3).

....

So What's a Chlorofluorocarbon?

Chlorofluorocarbons (CFCs) are nontoxic, non-flammable chemicals containing atoms of carbon, chlorine, and fluorine.

....

So What's Chlorine?

Chlorine is an element that is usually found as a gas. When it is used in swimming pools, it kills bacteria and prevents the growth of algae.

GREEN NEWS

In 1987 the United Nations Montreal Protocol agreement was passed to set limits on the release of CFCs by countries around the world. It is believed that this reduction of CFCs into the air will allow nature to repair this ozone hole to lower levels by 2065. But until then, higher levels of UV radiation will reach the earth's surface.

Protect Yourself Against UV Radiation

★ Wear UV-blocking sunglasses.

★ Limit your time in the sun between 10:00 AM and 4:00 PM when the rays of the sun are strongest.

★ Cover your body with tightly woven, loose-fitting clothing and a wide-brimmed hat.

★ Use a sunscreen with an SPF of at least 15. Apply the sunscreen thirty minutes before going out and reapply it every two hours. Reapply immediately after swimming, toweling off, or sweating a great deal.

The Issue:
Global Warming

Our earth is warmed by sunlight, but about 30 percent of the sunlight is reflected back into space. The remaining 70 percent of the light is absorbed by the land, air, and oceans, which heat our planet's surface and make life possible. As the rocks, air, and sea warm, they give off heat which travels back out to space, cooling the earth a bit.

Some of this outgoing heat, however, is absorbed by water vapor, carbon dioxide, and other gases in the atmosphere (called greenhouse gases because of their heat-trapping capacity). This heat is then radiated back toward the earth's surface. If there were no greenhouse gases or clouds in the atmosphere, the earth's average surface temperature would be a very chilly 0°F (18°C) instead of the comfortable 59°F (15°C).

Over the past 250 years, however, humans have raised the amount of carbon dioxide and methane in the atmosphere from power plants, factories, and automobiles. Even trash decomposing in landfills produces millions of pounds of methane. Most of these gases accumulate in the atmosphere.

Once these greenhouse gases move into the atmosphere, they stay for decades. Most scientists believe that the increased amount of greenhouse gases keep the heat from leaving the earth and has resulted in global warming.

DICTIONARY

So What's Global Warming?

Global warming is the term used for any rise in temperature of the earth's troposphere.

Temperature Shift

Scientists at the Mauna Loa laboratory in Hawaii have found that the amount of carbon dioxide in our air has increased by about one part per million every year for the last 50 years. Scientists believe the increase can be attributed to the large amounts of fossil fuels burned over the last 200 years. This increase of carbon dioxide may be a significant cause of global warming. Scientists have also found that the ten hottest years on record have occurred in the last 15 years.

We have seen temperature shifts throughout history; however, most of these small changes of only a few degrees have occurred over thousands of years. Now the rate of global warming is occurring at a much faster rate than ever before. Scientists are predicting a rise in the average temperature of the earth by 3°F to 10°F (1.7°–5.6°C) in your lifetime. That doesn't sound like much difference, but it can be compared with the climate change during the Ice Age when the world's temperature was only between 9°F (5°C) and 15°F (8.3°C) colder than today.

BE GREEN

Signs of Global Warming

Global warming and rising temperatures have led to glacier melting throughout the world. For instance, Greenland's glacier lost 100 billion metric tons of ice between 2003 and 2005. Scientists using data from the NASA/German Aerospace Center's Gravity Recovery and Climate Experiment (GRACE) have measured a significant decrease in the mass of the Greenland ice cap. These scientists have found that between the years of 2002 and 2005, Greenland's ice sheet decreased more than all previously published estimates.

Some other signs of global warming include the following indicators:

• Lack of ice is threatening the polar bear population. There has been a decline in the polar bear birthrate since the early 1980s, and adult polar bears are decreasing in weight.

• Our seasons are shifting. In Europe spring arrives between six and eight days earlier on average than in the 1970s, and 78 percent of 542 plant species have been found to flower and fruit earlier in the year. Migrating birds are returning to their northern homes earlier. The cherry blossoms in Washington DC are blooming earlier and earlier each spring.

• Many scientists believe the intense rainstorms we are seeing throughout the world are also a result of global warming.

• Scientists have discovered that carbon dioxide and methane are being released at a rate of 30 times faster than they were during a well-studied climate shift of 55 million years ago that triggered an extreme period of warming across the world.

DICTIONARY

So What's GRACE?

GRACE is a joint satellite mission between NASA and German Aerospace Center that measures movement in the earth's mass.

The disappearing glaciers are not confined to Greenland. Half of the glaciers in Spain that were present in 1980 have melted. China's glaciers, including those covering Mount Everest, are shrinking. And Siberia's permafrost has started to melt for the first time since it was formed at the end of the last ice age. Look on a globe. Can you locate the places where the glaciers are melting?

DICTIONARY

So What Are Emissions?

Emissions are greenhouse gases that are released into the atmosphere.

So What's a Glacier?

A *glacier* is a very large body of ice that moves very slowly down a slope or valley or spreads out in all directions. Glaciers are said to *advance* as they form or enlarge due to ice forming. When temperatures rise, glaciers are said to *retreat*, or melt.

So What's Permafrost?

Permafrost is a thick layer of soil below the surface that remains frozen throughout the year.

Help Stop Global Warming

TAKE ACTION

★ Ask a parent if you can plant more trees in your yard.

★ Suggest to your mom or dad that they turn the thermostat up in the summer and down in the winter. Ask your mom or dad to replace incandescent light bulbs with fluorescent bulbs.

★ Use public transportation and bicycles. Ask your parents to get regular tune-ups on their cars and keep their tires properly inflated. When shopping for a new family car, research hybrid cars and share what you learn with your parents.

★ Shop for items with less packaging, take reusable bags to the grocery store, and recycle as much as possible.

★ Learn all you can about global warming. Check out the Weather Channel's Forecast Earth web site (http://climate.weather.com/).

★ Go on the 30-Mile Diet. Food travels an average of 1,500 miles (2,414 km) before it reaches your table. Shop for food grown and produced within 30 miles (48 km) of your home. (Check out the 30-Mile Diet blog for more information at http://knowyourfarmer.livejournal.com/.)

Try This!

Take the global warming quiz on the National Audubon web site (http://www.audubon.org/globalWarming/quiz1.php) to see how much you know about the issue of global warming.

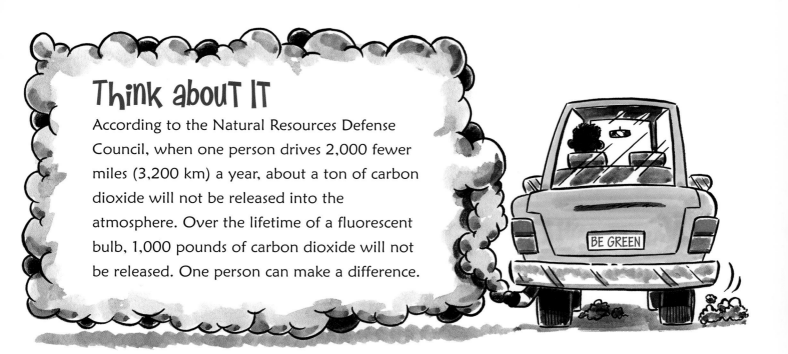

Think about It

According to the Natural Resources Defense Council, when one person drives 2,000 fewer miles (3,200 km) a year, about a ton of carbon dioxide will not be released into the atmosphere. Over the lifetime of a fluorescent bulb, 1,000 pounds of carbon dioxide will not be released. One person can make a difference.

GREEN NEWS

The town of Woodstock, New York, plans to erase the town's carbon footprint by the year 2017. The city has committed to reducing carbon dioxide emissions to zero within a decade. Their resolution lists ways to reach the zero-carbon goal including constructing green buildings, building bike paths, planting trees, and using biodiesel in city vehicles. Keep your eye on other towns and cities setting similar goals.

DICTIONARY

So What's a Green Building?

A *green building* uses construction techniques and materials that promote the well-being of the family, the community, and the environment.

Greenhouse EffecT

Create the greenhouse effect with this simple experiment.
You can also see this effect inside a car parked in the sun.

WhaT You Need

- **2 glass jars (large mayonnaise size)**
- **4 cups (1 L) water, divided**
- **6 ice cubes, divided**
- **Lid or clear plastic bag**
- **Thermometer**
- **Pencil and paper**

1 Fill each jar with 2 cups (0.5 L) of cold water and 3 ice cubes.

2 Cover one jar with a lid or plastic bag. Leave the other uncovered.

3 Place both jars in the sun for 1 hour.

4 Measure the temperature of the water in each jar, and write each down. Were they different?

DICTIONARY

So What's The Greenhouse Effect?

Have you ever visited a greenhouse where plants are grown? Was it warm? The *greenhouse effect* naturally occurs around our planet because carbon dioxide and other gases trap heat in our atmosphere.

Global warming, the rise in the earth's surface temperature, occurs when human activity increases the amount of the greenhouse gases in our atmosphere.

So What's A Carbon Footprint?

A *carbon footprint* is the measurement of all the greenhouse gases that a person, power source, or even a town produces in a year.

Try This! Visit the Native Energy site (http://www.nativeenergy.com/pages/carbon_footprint_calculator/41.php) to calculate your carbon dioxide emissions. What can you do every day to decrease those emissions?

Carbon Credits

The next time you attend a concert, you might be approached to buy carbon credits to offset the amount of carbon dioxide released into the atmosphere by all the fans driving to and from the concert in carbon dioxide–emitting vehicles. So what exactly are carbon credits, and how do they work? Do they erase the gases already emitted?

Well no, they do not erase the greenhouse emissions. Instead, according to the organization Native Energy, carbon credits can offset your carbon dioxide emissions by helping renewable projects, like wind turbines, to be built on tribal lands or family farms. Do you think this really does make a difference to global warming? You decide.

Melissa Poe

When Melissa Poe was nine years old, she watched a TV episode of *Highway to Heaven*, where Michael Landon, as an angel, provides a view of a future world with no trees and a lot of sickness. After the show, Michael Landon talked about the fact that each person can make a difference to the future.

Melissa believed she could make a difference too. She wrote a letter to President George H. W. Bush; that letter appeared on 250 billboards in April 1990. That's not all Melissa did. She started a club for other kids interested in taking action to make the future better. Melissa named the club Kids F.A.C.E. (Kids for a Clean Environment). Today, there are 2,000 chapters of Kids F.A.C.E. around the world with more than 300,000 members.

You can find out more about the club and how to start your own chapter in the Resources section. Melissa proved that no matter what age, each person has the ability to make a difference.

Eat More Vegetables

In 2006 the United Nations' Food and Agriculture Organization issued a report stating that the international meat industry generated 18 percent of the world's greenhouse gas emissions. Much of those gas emissions come from methane, a gas that is naturally produced during bovine (cattle) digestion, and nitrous oxide found in manure. Both methane and nitrous oxide gases have a warming effect that is greater than carbon. Methane is 23 times greater, and nitrous oxide is a whopping 296 times greater.

GREEN NEWS

New York City has begun a program called PLANYC that focuses on creating a greener city. The plan addresses changes in transportation, air, water, land use, energy, and climate change.

Taxis are already changing to hybrid automobiles that run on both gasoline and electricity. By the year 2012, all taxis in the city should be hybrid vehicles that get higher gas mileage than conventional vehicles. The city anticipates that by 2012 all taxis will average at least 30 miles (48 km) per gallon.

Because New York City residents generally have higher asthma rates than the national average, the city is also working on a plan to reduce the number of cars on the city streets by an average of 10,000 each day. The city hopes 94,000 people will take buses and trains to help clear up auto congestion and air pollution. The Congestion Pricing Plan, as the new plan is called, would require drivers to pay eight dollars per day to drive into certain areas of the city.

Other plans call for planting one million trees. Hurray for the Big Apple!

DICTIONARY

So What's a Hybrid car?

A *hybrid car* uses an alternative fuel, like electricity, along with gasoline.

Try This!

Find out if your city or the city nearest you is becoming "green." Many cities are stepping up and creating their own initiatives. If your city has begun a green campaign, write a letter to the mayor to applaud some of the steps the city is taking to become "green."

The Issue: Light Pollution

The Milky Way is dimming, not because the end of the universe is near, but rather as a result of light pollution from street lights, outdoor advertising, homes, schools, airports, and other sources. Every night billions of bulbs send their energy skyward where microscopic bits of matter reflect much of the wasted light back to earth.

If there is so much light from buildings and streetlights that you can no longer see the stars in the night sky, we say there is light pollution. But

does this kind of pollution affect us? Biologists think it does. For instance, light pollution is blamed by some scientists for the decline of sea turtles because the female lays her eggs in the dark. The light not only affects their nesting habits, but it also interferes with the young hatchlings who need the moonlight to find their way to the sea, not back to a lighted building.

In addition, biologists now are studying many nocturnal creatures that thrive in blackness. More than 450 bird species use the moon and stars for navigation during their biannual migrations. Biologists believe that when these birds fly through a brightly lit area, they can actually become disoriented and crash into brilliantly lit buildings. They sometimes even circle these buildings until they drop from exhaustion. Sometimes whole flocks fly into brightly lit objects.

Research has not yet been concluded on animals like bats and moths who thrive in darkness. As yet, we don't know how these nocturnal animals will be affected, but we can be sure that they will be affected in some way.

Keep a Dark Sky

★ Replace the high wattage light bulbs outside your house with low wattage bulbs to reduce stray light.

★ Celebrate National Dark-Sky Week in April of each year during the week of the new moon, since a full moon increases the light pollution. This is the perfect time to host a star party.

★ Find out if there is a lighting code in your community. Your town hall should be able to answer your question, but bring along a grownup when you ask. If there is no lighting code, encourage the city officials to develop one.

★ If your community abides by certain lighting codes, it might qualify as an International Dark-Sky Community. Check out the Association's web site to nominate your community: http://www.darksky.org.

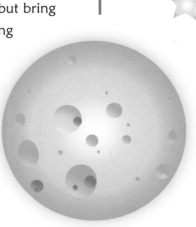

WATER

"When the well is dry we know the worth of water."

—Benjamin Franklin

Water, Water Everywhere, But Not a Drop To Drink

Benjamin Franklin was right; sometimes you don't know the worth of something until it is gone. Fortunately this is not the case with the earth's water, but we must conserve the world's freshwater.

First and foremost we need fresh, clean water for drinking; but we also need water for crop irrigation, navigation, hydroelectric power, industry, recreation, and for wildlife. Just think of all the ways you use water each day. The demands for freshwater continue to challenge our planet's freshwater supply even though water is the most abundant liquid on earth. Although water covers two-thirds of the earth, freshwater represents only 0.1 percent of all water. Freshwater is found in ground water, lakes, glaciers, and icebergs.

Each of us can make a difference in keeping our water clean. Read on to learn how you can help.

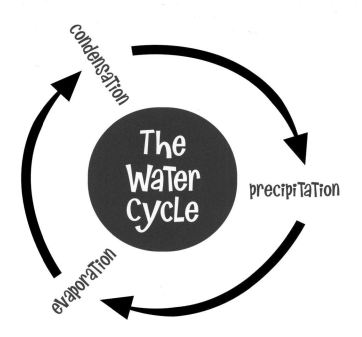

The
Water
Cycle

condensation

precipitation

evaporation

SCIENCE SPEAK

The Water Cycle

The water cycle, or *hydrologic* cycle, is the continuing process of water being exchanged among clouds, land, and oceans. Molecules of water from the surface of the ocean and land are warmed by the sun and evaporate into the air as water vapor. At the higher altitude's lower temperature and air pressure, water vapor condenses into precipitation, such as rain or snow. The precipitation falls to earth, where about seven-eighths fall directly into the ocean and only the remaining one-eighth of the total precipitation falls on land.

DICTIONARY

So What's Evaporation?

Evaporation is the process of water changing from a liquid to a vapor.

....

So What's Condensation?

Condensation is the process of water changing from a vapor to a liquid.

....

So What's Precipitation?

When water vapor, which has condensed in the atmosphere, becomes too heavy to remain in atmospheric air currents, it falls as *precipitation* in the form of rain, snow, sleet, or hail.

DON'T TREAD ON ME

Make a Water Cycle in a Jar

What You Need

- **Gravel**
- **Wide-mouthed jar**
- **Peat moss**
- **Soil**
- **Violet or fern plant**
- **Plastic wrap**
- **Rubber band**

1 Place a 1-inch (2.5 cm) layer of gravel in the bottom of the jar. Add 1 inch (2.5 cm) of peat moss, then a layer of soil.

2 Plant the violet or fern in the soil and water lightly.

3 Cover the mouth of the jar with plastic wrap and secure with a rubber band.

4 Watch the water molecules condense on the glass and "rain" back into the jar. You've created your very own indoor water cycle.

Find The Source of Your Water Supply

★ Find out where your water comes from.

★ Try to visit the waterworks in your community to learn how your water is cleaned and treated to make it safe to drink.

The Issue: Pure Water

When you turn on the tap inside your house, do you know where that water comes from? In most large cities, the water comes from surface water sources, such as reservoirs, rivers, and lakes. These sources might be close to your home or far away. In smaller towns or rural areas, drinking water may come from wells that tap into aquifers that might only be a few miles wide or cover many states.

Activities many miles away from your water source may affect the quality of your drinking water. Factories many miles upstream from the water source may pollute the drinking water by dumping pollutants into streams and rivers. Even run-off from farms may seep into aquifers. All can pollute the drinking water in your area.

DICTIONARY

So What's an Aquifer?

An *aquifer* is a natural water reservoir under the earth's surface

The Waterkeepers

The waterkeeper program began in 1960 to protect the Hudson River but led to the creation of more than 120 waterkeeper programs all over the world. The waterkeepers include riverkeepers, coastkeepers, baykeepers, and streamkeepers who advocate on behalf of the waters they protect. They act as educators, scientists, coalition builders, investigators, spokespeople, and visionaries. They rely on many people to help them, including environmental experts, lawyers, local fishermen, and community volunteers. All of us can watch for changes in the water near our homes. If you spot possible pollution, report it to a local waterkeeper. Our waterkeepers are all Earth Heroes! (Find out more at http://www.waterkeeper.org.)

IT Happened in The Past: A River Burned

1969 JUNE

On June 22, 1969, the Cuyahoga River in Cleveland, Ohio, caught fire and burned for 30 minutes. This was not the first time the river had burned; it was the tenth time! Factories up the river dumped pollutants into it, but with the fire in 1969, the people of Cleveland had had enough. This time the fire helped lead to the passage of the Clean Water Act of 1972.

Cuyahoga River Fire, June 22, 1969

The Clean Water Act of 1972

Surface-water quality is protected in the United States through the Clean Water Act, designed to sharply reduce direct pollutants into our waterways. The Clean Water Act has made it mandatory for cities to clean up municipal sewage plants and industrial facilities. With those facilities cleaned up, attention has turned to controlling polluted run-off from construction sites and farms.

Ground-Water Filter Experiment

What You Need

- **4 plastic 1-gallon (4 L) milk jugs**
- **Rubber bands**
- **Cheesecloth**
- **4 different types of soil: clay, sand, woodland soil, peat moss**
- **4 large glass jars**
- **Scissors**
- **Stop watch or clock with second hand**
- **2 cups (0.5 L) water, divided**
- **Pencil and paper**

1 Ask a grownup to remove the bottoms of the plastic jugs.

2 Use the rubber bands to secure a piece of cheesecloth to the top of each jug. Turn the jugs upside down so the cheese-cloth ends rest inside the jars.

3 Fill each jug ⅔ full with a different soil.

4 Pour about ½ cup (118 ml) of water into each bottle and record the time it takes for the water to filter through the soil into the jar.

5 Repeat for each of the soil samples.

6 Which soil allowed the water to flow the fastest? Which jar has the most water? Which soil would you select for a garden? Why?

DICTIONARY

So What's Ground Water?

Precipitation may soak into the soil, be absorbed by plants, or run off land surfaces into streams and lakes. Water not absorbed by plants will eventually become *groundwater* underneath the surface of the earth.

The Issue:
Water Shortages

As the world's population grows, global consumption of water for industries and agriculture grows as well, and there is a growing need for more and more water. Water ultimately comes from precipitation, but rain is not always guaranteed. Some months have less rain than other months; and there are periods of drought in many areas of the world.

Scientists are looking at several solutions to water shortages. One solution to the problem is the construction of dams across rivers or streams. The dam interrupts the flow of water and collects it in a reservoir or lake. This water is then controlled and used when needed.

Other engineers and scientists are trying to develop new sources of water. One method is desalinization, which removes salt from sea water and makes the water drinkable. So far, however, this process is too costly to be used on a large scale.

Another solution to water shortages is conservation of the water we have. This is an area in which we can all help.

Try This!

If the average family of four showered each day for five minutes, they would use 700 gallons (2,650 L) of water in one week. How much extra water would the family use if each of them took 15-minute showers? How long do you shower?

DICTIONARY

So What's a Reservoir?

A *reservoir* is a natural or man-made lake or pond that stores water to use.

Try This!

Fill a clean, one-gallon jug (4 L) with water and challenge yourself to use only that water for a day. See if you can use that water to brush your teeth, wash your hands and face, and drink.

Conserve Water

★ Take short showers.

★ Install a low-flow showerhead.

★ Turn off the faucet while you brush your teeth.

★ When you have finished with your water, make sure you firmly turn off the faucet.

★ Don't use your toilet as a trash can.

★ Rather than running the faucet every time you want a cold drink of water, fill a clean jug with water and keep it in your refrigerator during the day.

★ Save the clean water used for rinsing dishes for watering plants, or catch rainwater and use it to water the plants.

DON'T TREAD ON ME

Hold a Town Meeting

What if you lived in an area suffering from severe drought, and water was in very limited supply? Try your hand at conducting a town meeting with your friends to come up with a water-rationing plan for your town that would limit everyone's water use.

What You Need
- **Several friends or a school class**
- **Pen and paper**
- **Poster board**
- **Markers**

1 Discuss the water shortage with your friends or class.

2 Make a list of water conservation rules and water rationing that can be put in force in your town.

3 Create a poster illustrating the rules.

4 How would you let your town citizens know about the new rules? Decide how your town would enforce the new water rules.

GREEN NEWS

The city of San Francisco has stopped buying bottled water for municipal employees. This creates less trash in the landfills, cuts down on the oil needed to create the plastic bottles, and reduces the carbon dioxide released during plastic bottle production. Encourage your city government to switch to tap water instead of buying bottled water.

The Issue: Bottled Water

Visit a supermarket and you'll find many types of bottled water for sale. There's water from natural springs, purified water, water with vitamins, water with flavorings and many more. In 2001 Americans bought five billion gallons of bottled water, according to the International Bottled Water Association (IBWA). That's just about two hours of water from the American Falls at Niagara Falls.

The U.S. Food and Drug Administration (FDA) regulates bottled water as a packaged food and has established standards of quality and manufacturing practice requirements for the processing and bottling of drinking water.

GREEN NEWS

Instead of buying plastic bottles filled with water, there are many ways to filter your own tap water. Some filters attach to the faucet and filter water as it comes through the tap. Other filters are attached to a container and the water is poured through the filter. Either way, these filters provide good-tasting water, and you'll save money. And you'll save the earth from plastic bottles.

Stop Using Bottled Water

TAKE ACTION

★ Drink tap water.

★ Fill up reusable bottles with cold tap water instead of purchasing individual bottles.

★ If you must use bottled water, at least recycle the polyethylene terephthalate (PET) water bottles you use. This will eliminate the air pollution created when your bottles are burned with regular trash.

DON'T TREAD ON ME

The Issue:
Beach Closings

It's been more than 30 years since the first Earth Day ignited the nation's interest in our environment, but we still face some of the same problems. Chicago ordered 34 beach closings on Lake Michigan during the summer of 2007, and Chicago wasn't alone. A record number of beach closings and warnings were issued that year across the country, according to a report by the Natural Resources Defense Council. In 2006 more than 1,600 beaches were temporarily closed or had warnings posted because of high bacteria levels. In spite of the attention and the beach cleanups, there is still a problem with our beaches. Why?

Storm water run-off seems to be a major source of this problem, causing 10,597 advisory or closing days in 2006. During heavy rains, debris, waste, and pollution from cities and towns flow with the water into the coastal areas. This seems to be the case in the city of Chicago.

DICTIONARY

So What's Run-Off?

Run-off is water that flows on the surface or through the ground into streams, lakes, rivers, and oceans.

Stay Safe and Fight Beach Pollution

TAKE ACTION

★ Avoid swimming after a heavy rainfall.

★ Try not to swallow the swim water.

★ Leave the water immediately if you see any waste or pollution.

★ Shower after you leave the beach.

★ Hold a beach cleanup party.

★ Make sure the babies you know wear plastic pants when they visit the beach.

★ Clean up after your dog when walking it on the beach.

★ Always dispose of household toxins properly.

DON'T TREAD ON ME

The Issue: Oil Spills

Oil spills are always a threat to our rivers and oceans. A small amount of oil naturally flows into the ocean from underneath the sea floor; but that oil is such a small amount that the bacteria in the ocean feed on the carbon in the oil and break it down. When a large tanker carrying oil has an accident and spills barrels of oil all at once, the bacteria in the sea cannot break it down fast enough.

The oil floats on the surface of the water and creates a life-threatening situation for wildlife and the environment. The oil coats the feathers of seabirds, so that the birds are unable to fly or swim. Oil clogs the hair of animals like otters and seals and they freeze to death. Fish can die from ingesting oil, and humans can get sick from eating fish with oil in their bodies. Oil damages fish eggs, larvae, and young fish and harms the food chain for many generations. The death toll is high for wildlife after an oil spill.

Don't Add Oil To Our Water Supply

★ Never dump oil in sewers or down a drain. The run-off will take the oil to our streams and oceans.

★ Avoid using oil by riding your bike or walking.

★ If there is an oil spill near you, volunteer to help in the cleanup.

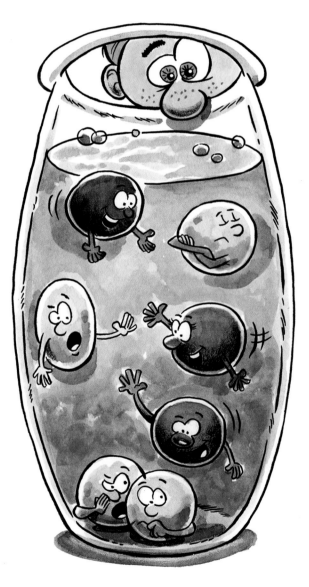

SCIENCE SPEAK

Oil and Water

Just like the oil and vinegar in a bottle of salad dressing, oil and water don't mix. Even if you shake the bottle up, the two layers will separate again after they settle. Did you ever wonder why they don't mix? If it were up to the oil molecules they would, but the water molecules are a bit more standoffish. They like to stick to their own kind. Water molecules are so attracted to each other they do not allow the oil molecules to mix in between them. The oil is less dense than the water, which causes the oil molecules to float on the water's surface. This is why oil spills are so hard to clean up.

DON'T TREAD ON ME

IT Happened in the Past: The *Exxon Valdez* Oil Spill

March 24, 1989, the oil tanker *Exxon Valdez*, owned by the oil company Exxon, left the oil terminal of Valdez, Alaska, carrying 53 million gallons of crude oil bound for California. The tanker struck Bligh Reef in Alaska's Prince William Sound, and 11 million gallons of oil leaked into the sea. Within two months, the oil had been driven along a path stretching 470 miles (756 km) to the southwest. The initial cleanup of the spill took three years, and the cost was over $2.1 billion. The death toll in terms of wildlife was staggering, and the full impact may never be known.

As a result of the *Exxon Valdez* disaster, tighter environmental regulations have been imposed on many industries. The most important regulation attempting to protect against a repeat of the oil spill is that tanker ships must now be built with double hulls. If the outer hull is punctured, no oil will leak.

Not all oil spills are from tankers. In 2007 a cargo ship hit a bridge in San Francisco Bay and lost 58,000 gallons of oil. Nearly 400 birds died as a result of the oil spill.

Oil-covered sea lions take a break in Prince William Sound.

CLean Up The SpiLL

Here's a way to test some of the strategies used in cleaning up oil spills.

WhaT You Need
- **Baking pan**
- **Water**
- **4 tablespoons (60 ml) oil**
- **Twine**
- **Paper towel**
- **Straw**

1 Fill the bottom of the baking pan with water.

2 Pour oil onto the water. Watch as two layers form.

3 Now try to clean up the layer of oil. First use a length of twine positioned on top of the water in an attempt to keep the oil spill enclosed. Does the barrier work to isolate the oil from the rest of the water?

4 Try to blot the oil with the paper towel.

5 Experiment with a straw. Try to extract the oil by placing one end of the straw in the oil and use your finger to close off the other and lift the oil out.

6 What other methods could you use for removing the oil?

7 Which method was the most successful at removing the oil? Can you imagine a spill that consists of more than 11 million gallons of oil?

Iceberg Ecology

Seventy-nine percent of our freshwater is contained in glaciers and icebergs. Both are melting due to increased global warming, but nature is full of twists and turns. Icebergs have broken free from Antarctica in the Weddell Sea and, as they melt, may actually be reversing the buildup of green-house gases in our atmosphere. These icebergs are also creating a whole new area of sea life and their own ecology.

Iceberg ice isn't as pure and clean as many thought. Over thousands of years, iceberg ice has picked up minerals, including iron, which along with nutrients set off a new food chain beginning with tiny phytoplankton. The chlorophyll-rich phytoplankton make the water green as they absorb carbon dioxide and produce oxygen. Krill find all that phytoplankton a regular buffet. Other creatures, like jellies, move in to feed on the krill. Other sea creatures feed on the jellies and the feeding moves up the food chain. Only a small percentage of krill are eaten. The rest die and take with them carbon dioxide pulled from the atmosphere.

DICTIONARY

So What's Phytoplankton?

Phytoplankton are microscopic plants that float on the water.

Phytoplankton bloom all along the coast of Southeast United States.

GREEN NEWS

In 2004 researchers seeded part of the ocean with iron to see if a bloom of phytoplankton would develop. It did indeed! The phytoplankton that bloomed consumed more than 30,000 tons of carbon dioxide. Scientists continue to examine the use of iron and phytoplankton to combat global warming.

DON'T TREAD ON ME

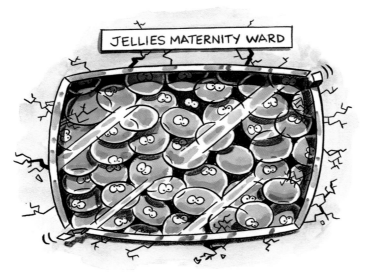

JELLIES MATERNITY WARD

Jellies Population Increasing

When any population increases in an ecosystem, there is cause for alarm. For the last few years, there has been an expansion of the population of jellyfish in the oceans. A report in 2002 stated an increase in box jellies off the coast of Hawaii. Smacks of jellies off the coast of France have sunk 500-pound (227 kg) fishing nets. In 2005 residents of Marco Island, Florida, complained about the stinging jellies in their waters. Jellies are clogging water intakes at power plants, and some of these creatures are 400 pounds (181 kg).

Scientists studied these blooms and posed the explanation that overfishing and changes in the ocean environment may be decreasing the amount of fish in the ocean, creating a gap for the jellies to fill. Jellies like warm waters filled with phytoplankton to eat.

Japanese researchers are working on developing uses for the jellies. They are experimenting with extracting a protein substance called *mucin*. Mucins lubricate parts of our body and also have antibacterial qualities. The jellyfish mucins may be able to be used in drug delivery, cosmetics, food products, and other products.

No-Sting Jelly

Jellies are about 95 percent water. Here's how you can create your own model jelly that won't sting you.

What You Need

- **2 clear, sealable plastic bags**
- **Water**
- **Liquid food coloring**
- **Bag tie**

1 Fill one plastic bag about half full of water.

2 Add 1 drop of food coloring.

3 Add just a little water to the second bag and push it inside the first bag to create the stomach of the jelly.

4 Tie the two bags together with a bag tie and carefully turn the bags over. Tuck in the corners.

5 Place your jelly model in a basin of water and watch it float.

Dr. Carl Berg

EARTH HERO

Dr. Carl Berg is a marine ecologist and long-time water-quality champion who lives in Hanalei Bay, Kauai, Hawaii. When he moved to Hawaii in 1990, Dr. Berg worked as a beach and stream water-quality monitor. He helped start a monitoring system for the beaches, river, and streams of Hanalei Bay for bacteria, and he set up volunteers to track bacterial sources. He later formed the Hanalei Watershed Hui. (*Hui* is the Hawaiian word for *group.*) The Watershed Hui worked to remove cesspools on and near beach parks and along rivers that flowed into the bay. Dr. Berg continues to make Hawaii's beaches cleaner.

DON'T TREAD ON ME

The Issue:
PCBs PoLLuTion

Many rivers, such as the Hudson River in New York, the Fox River in Wisconsin, the Housatonic River in Massachusetts, and the Kalamazoo River in Michigan, are polluted by PCBs. Sometimes PCBs were dumped into the river by manufacturing plants. Other times, PCBs leaked from hazardous waste sites and entered the groundwater through run-off. When PCBs enter a river, they become part of the food chain. Small organisms in the river absorb them. Fish and other river creatures eat the smaller organisms and threaten the whole ecosystem.

Scientists, corporations, and conservationists have been working for years on the best ways to clean up PCBs from our rivers and communities. They have dredged rivers to scoop the PCBs out of the river sediment and experimented with PCB-eating microbes. There is hope now that an enzyme found in earthworms can break down PCBs.

SCIENCE SPEAK

PCBs

The letters PCB stand for *polychlorinated biphenyls*, a mixture of dangerous compounds that were once used as coolants and lubricants in transformers, capacitors, and other electrical equipment. PCBs are no longer made in the United States. Their production was stopped in 1977 because their accumulation can cause health problems, and they don't break down in the environment.

Fish for Information

★ Look for warning signs posted along the water's edge. If there are signs, follow the advice printed on them.

★ Even if you don't see warning signs, call your local or state health agencies or the EPA and ask for their advice. Ask them if there are any advisories on the kinds or sizes of fish that may be eaten from the waters where you plan to fish. You can also ask about fishing advisories at local sporting goods or bait shops where fishing licenses are sold.

★ Take home and eat the smaller, younger fish (within legal limits) of lake trout, salmon, walleye, and bass. Younger fish are less likely to contain harmful levels of pollutants than the larger, older fish.

★ Eat panfish, such as bluegill, perch, stream trout, and smelt. These species feed on insects and other aquatic life and are less likely to contain high levels of harmful pollutants.

★ Avoid taking home fatty fish, such as lake trout, or fish that feed on the bottoms of lakes and streams such as catfish and carp. These fish are more likely to contain higher levels of chemical pollutants.

How To Safely Clean Fresh Fish

PCBs are mainly stored in the fat and can be reduced by getting rid of the fat located along the back, belly, and dark meat along the side of the fish. Skinning the fish will remove the thin layer of fat under the skin. Trim the fat, remove the skin, and fillet the fish before cooking. When cooking, use a method such as baking or grilling that allows the juices to drain away. Throw away the cooking juices.

The Issue:
Fish Farming

When you hear "fish farming," do you have visions of a farm with fish growing in rows and rows? No, fish farms, called *aquaculture*, are sometimes in the coastal waters of the ocean and sometimes inland. Whether fish farming is good for the environment, or bad, depends on which fish are farmed, how they are raised, and where the farm is located.

Farm-raised oysters, clams, and mussels are good choices. Clams are farmed in special beds on sandy beaches, where their harvest does little to disturb the ecosystem. Oysters and mussels are usually raised in cages suspended off the seafloor; they filter tiny plankton out of the water for their food. These shellfish can even improve water quality as they clear the water of excess plankton. Since oysters, clams, and mussels must come from non-polluted water when farmed for human consumption, these farms are interested in keeping the ocean clean.

Other farmed fish, including most farmed salmon, are raised in net pens. In these pens are thousands of fish polluting the water. And since salmon are carnivores (meat eaters), they must be fed food made from other fish caught in the wild. So fish food for these species actually creates more demand for wild fish! Raising fish that are herbivores (plant eaters) is an easier task.

Tilapia is a plant-eating fish that is easy to raise and does not need wild fish as feed. Tilapia, catfish, and trout are all raised inland; and these fish can be delicious alternatives to ocean-farmed fish. Experiments are now being conducted so that someday all fish farming can be moved inland, where wastes would be easier to handle.

Eat Only Vegetarian Seafood

★ Eat these farm-raised fish:

Arctic char	oysters
barramundi	bay scallops
catfish	striped bass
clams	tilapia
mussels	rainbow trout

★ Avoid these farm-raised fish:

salmon

shrimp

★ Download a seafood guide from the Monterrey Bay Aquarium and share it with your parents. http://www.mbayaq.org/cr/cr_seafoodwatch/sfw_consumers.asp

The Issue: Overfishing

It is hard to believe that the fish served on restaurant menus could be endangered. After all, there are at least 20,000 species of fish in the ocean. The ocean is huge, so how can there be any shortage? Unfortunately, restaurant menus do not show the full picture. Between 1950 and 1994, ocean fishermen increased their fish catch 400 percent. In 1989 the world's catch was just over 82 million metric tons of fish per year. That's all the fish the oceans can produce.

Now many fish species are in danger, and some of the problems stem from fishing methods. When commercial fishermen locate the fish they are looking for, often their methods of catching them are not selective, meaning they catch a lot of other creatures—like sea turtles, diving birds, and dolphins—in addition to the fish they are after. Those

creatures that end up in the nets and lines are called *bycatch*. According to the United Nations Food and Agriculture Organization, one in four animals caught in fishing gear dies as bycatch. That's thousands of tons of fish being thrown away each year.

DICTIONARY

So What's Marine Stewardship Certification?

Marine Stewardship Certification (MSC) is an internationally recognized set of environmental principles for measuring fisheries to assess if they are well managed and sustainable.

....

So What's Bycatch?

The *bycatch* is ocean wildlife caught along with the species of fish desired. This includes young fish, other fish species, sea turtles, ocean birds, and mammals.

....

So What's Overfishing?

Overfishing is catching fish faster than the fish have time to reproduce.

Eat Only Ocean-Friendly Seafood

★ Look for seafood with the seal of Marine Stewardship Certification (MSC). This seal ensures that the conservation of fish populations is followed. Their label is a white fish on a blue background. If you don't see it, ask the grocery store to buy fish with the label.

★ Talk to your parent about buying fish lower on the food chain, like mackerel, clams, and squid. They are more plentiful than the top ocean predators of shark, tuna, and swordfish.

★ If you ever have the opportunity to eat caviar, avoid the caviar from wild sturgeons. Their population is in danger.

★ Visit your local fish market and ask them about their fish. Find out if the salmon they sell is farm-raised, if their clams are gathered by dredging the ocean floor, or if their shrimp is harvested by trawling. These practices are all ecologically damaging to the fish and the environment.

★ Check the list of supermarket chains that sell seafood with the MSC logo (see http://eng.msc.org/). If your supermarket is not listed, write a letter to the supermarket headquarters and explain to them your concern about the fish they sell. Tell them why some fishing methods are damaging to ocean and marine animals.

DON'T TREAD ON ME

DICTIONARY

So What's Trawling?

Trawling is catching fish using a cone-shaped net that is dragged through the water or along the bottom of the ocean.

....

So What's Long Lining?

Long lining fishermen extend a long cable into the ocean with many baited hooks. Other ocean creatures may be caught on the hooks.

Groupers. There are over 85 species of groupers (also called sea bass), all of which are vulnerable to overfishing because they spawn together in the same places every year. Groupers can live up to 40 years, but they reproduce only for a short period of time, which makes them especially vulnerable to overfishing. Many groupers sold in the United States come from the Gulf of Mexico where fishing management has been poor.

Atlantic Bluefin Tuna. This is the most valuable fish for sushi, a growing food trend in the U.S. This species has been listed as critically endangered since 1996. But because the bluefin tuna migrates between the Pacific, Atlantic, and Mediterranean Oceans, fishing control is difficult to police. Fishermen use a variety of ways to catch tuna, including harpoons, traps, long lines, and nets that entangle sea turtles, seabirds, and sharks

Atlantic Cod. Many years of overfishing has depleted the cod population so drastically that it shows no sign of rebuilding. The bottom trawling that is used to catch cod also destroys valuable ocean habitat.

Some Solutions To Bycatching

Fishermen don't like it when they unload a load of bycatch. It wastes their time and money, so scientists and engineers are designing new fishing gear to eliminate bycatch. Some of these new innovations include electronic beepers placed on fishnets to warn sea mammals of the nets. A turtle excluder device, or TED, is a trap door in shrimp nets that lets turtles swim free. Fishermen who use long lines now fish at night when birds are sleeping or have special lines that scare away sea birds.

Fish Harvesting Machines

Sometimes fish are "harvested." The harvesting machine is combined with a pump that attracts fish and squid with a light and then sucks them up onto the deck of the boat. Unfortunately, only small fish can be harvested in this way without injury.

Try This!

Download a copy of Audubon's *Living Ocean's Seafood Lover's Guide* to help you make seafood choices that will keep our oceans healthy. Find your guide at http://seafood.audubon.org/.

Coral and Coral Reefs

Corals are invertebrate animals belonging to a large group of colorful animals called *cnidaria* (nee-DAR-ee-ah). Other animals in this group include jellyfish and sea anemones. Each individual coral animal is called a *polyp*. Thousands of identical polyps live in groups that form a colony. The colony is formed by a process called *budding*, which is when the original polyp literally grows copies of itself.

There are hard and soft corals. Hard corals extract calcium from seawater and create a hardened structure for themselves that provides protection. Millions of hard coral polyps form large calcium structures called *coral reefs*. Coral reefs are the largest living structure on earth and the only living structure visible from space. Coral reefs are rich in marine life. More than one-quarter of the 500,000 marine animal species in the world call reefs home. Scientists are even exploring coral reef bacteria for naturally occurring antibiotics. Who knows what other cures may be found in ocean reefs?

DICTIONARY

So What's Dredging?

Dredging is scraping the ocean floor to harvest clams, mussels, and other shellfish. This process damages the ocean habitat.

Coral polyps in a coral colony

The Issue:
Dying Coral Reefs

Coral reefs all over the world are in danger from pollution, human activities, and temperature changes. Climate conditions are considered a major factor in coral reef health as is increased population. When land is cleared for housing and farming, silt and topsoil flow into the ocean, covering and killing the coral. Sewage and fertilizers also flow into the ocean and create algae which smother the coral.

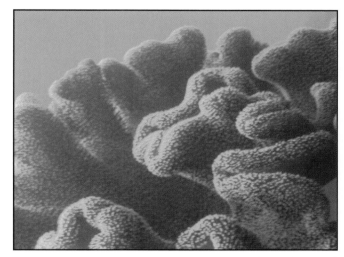

A massive coral

Protect Coral Reefs

★ If you purchase aquarium fish or corals, make sure they are aquaculture-raised and harvested.

★ Do not throw your trash into the ocean.

★ When diving or snorkeling, look, but do not touch, coral.

★ When boating in the ocean, never cast your anchor on or run aground on a coral reef.

★ Buy natural pesticides and fertilizers instead of ones that are chemically treated.

DICTIONARY

So What's Bleaching?

Bleaching occurs when ocean temperatures reach their warmest levels, usually in late summer and early fall. During the strong El Niño of 1998, about 30 percent of coral off the Florida Keys died after a single mass bleaching.

DON'T TREAD ON ME

Land

"The clearest way into the Universe is through a forest wilderness."
—John Muir

O Give Me Land, Lots of Land

Imagine a time when our country was unexplored and unpolluted, when Native Americans lived in harmony with the land. We can still get a glimpse of wild America, especially in our national parks. There are ocean cliffs and beaches, mountains that touch the clouds, and streams that meander through flowered meadows. You can stand at the edge of the Grand Canyon or the top of Yosemite's Glacier Point and imagine you are the first person to discover its beauty and vastness. Or you might take a walk with your family in a nearby park and be able to sit in silence, hearing just the wind blowing the leaves overhead and the birds calling to each other.

So, if there is all this beauty around and open space, why are we so concerned? With the worldwide population increasing, there is more and more waste to be disposed of, most of which ends up in our landfills. Not only does all this waste take up space, often toxins from household garbage and industry seep into the land and can poison it. To prevent the earth from becoming polluted, we must all practice good conservation methods and reduce our waste, recycle what we can, and reuse rather than buying new.

DICTIONARY

So What's Land Pollution?

Land pollution is a poisoning of the earth through herbicides and pesticides, industrial waste dumping, and poor waste disposal.

John Muir

John Muir is often referred to as "The Father of our National Parks." Born in Scotland in 1838, he moved to America with his family when he was about ten years old. Muir walked 1,000 miles from Indianapolis to the Gulf of Mexico and eventually ended up in the Sierra Nevadas and Yosemite, California.

Muir's writings, enthusiasm, and efforts led to the creation of Yosemite National Park on October 1, 1890. Muir was also personally involved in the creation of Sequoia, Mount Rainier, Petrified Forest, and Grand Canyon national parks. In 1892 Muir founded the Sierra Club, through which Muir's vision and legacy endures. In 1908 President Theodore Roosevelt designated an ancient redwood forest just north of San Francisco as the Muir Woods National Monument. Upon receiving the honor, Muir wrote: "This is the best tree-lover's monument that could possibly be found in all the forests of the world."

Seventh Generation

The Iroquois inspired the belief that you should always make decisions based on their impact on the seventh generation. In other words, how will your decision impact your great, great, great, great, great-grandchild?

The Issue:
Trash and Waste

According to the Clean Air Council, each American generates over four pounds (1.8 kg) of trash per day and up to 56 tons of trash per year. Only about one-tenth of that trash gets recycled; the rest ends up in landfills. Roughly one-third of our trash comes just from packaging. Look around your house and take a look at what you will recycle and what will end up in your trash. Take a look at your house during the holiday season. Talk about trash! We generate an extra five million tons of waste just during the holidays. All this waste is not paper and plastic; it's also food. The waste doesn't stop there. We dispose of roughly 20,000 cars each day and 65 billion soda cans each year.

There are things we throw away all the time that are not biodegradable, meaning that the waste will stay in our environment without breaking down. Let's explore ways to reduce, reuse, and recycle trash.

Check with your city's waste-management office to find out what items you can recycle and how you should separate them. Set up plastic bins to store your recyclables. Label each bin to indicate what recyclable you will store there. For example, label one bin CARDBOARD AND PAPER, another GLASS, the next PLASTICS, and the next CANS. Ask your family to put these items in the bins. Ask a grownup to take the bins to a recycling center each week.

Reduce, Reuse, Recycle

TAKE ACTION

★ Reduce, because the best way to manage waste is not to produce it at all.

★ Reuse, because this keeps goods out of landfills and incinerators and reduces the need for raw materials to make new goods.

★ Recycle, because it is what you can do everyday to protect the environment, save energy, and conserve natural resources.

Is there an area of your community that seems to collect trash? Get together with your scout troop, classmates, or friends and plan a community cleanup day. Advertise with posters around town. Always use gloves and find out the safest way to remove items. Ask grownups to help you to dispose of the trash you remove. Bring recyclables to a redemption center. Celebrate your results with a community picnic.

DICTIONARY

So What's Biodegradable?

Biodegradable is an object that can be broken down naturally by living organisms.

....

So What's a Landfill?

A *landfill* is a large outdoor area where waste is disposed and covered with thin layers of soil each day.

IT Happened in The Past: Love Canal, NY

1978 AUGUST

Love Canal, New York, began as a dream community on the eastern edge of Niagara Falls. William Love built a canal to join the upper and lower Niagara Rivers so the community would have cheap power. But when the money ran out, Love Canal was left with a big ditch. By the 1920s, the canal became a dumping ground for city and industry wastes; and by 1953, the owner of the canal covered the whole thing with dirt and sold it to the city of Love Canal for $1.00. One hundred homes went up. People moved in. A school was built. When a record amount of rainfall fell in 1978, toxic-waste disposal drums pushed through the grounds of backyards. Today Love Canal is a polluted ghost town.

Since Love Canal, the Environmental Protection Agency has worked to provide clean air, water, and soil standards for the U.S. and to enforce these standards so there will be no more Love Canals.

The EPA posting at a polluted site similar to that of Love Canal

Chad Pregracke

Chad Pregracke grew up beside the Mississippi River. By the time he reached high school, he became aware that trash littered the river. In 1997 while in college, Chad tried to get government funding for a cleanup. When he could not get federal help, he set about to clean up the river himself, one piece of garbage at a time. In 1998 Chad founded an organization he named Living Lands & Waters. Today, Chad has several employees and a fleet of barges and workboats. Thousands of volunteers have helped with the community cleanups. Volunteers have pulled out roughly four million tons of trash in river areas. The haul might include old refrigerators, bowling balls, dolls, car parts, and even bones. Although community cleanups are the thrust of the organization, other programs include educational workshops, Riverbottom Forest Restoration, and an Adopt-a-Mississippi-Mile program. Chad was a kid with a vision and he has made a difference. Find out more at http://www.livinglandsandwaters.org.

Batteries Are Special

Laptops, walkmans, toys, cell phones, and calculators are just some of the things that use batteries. The EPA estimates that more than 350 million rechargeable batteries are purchased annually in the United States. Batteries are a unique product comprised of heavy metals and other elements that make things "portable" but can threaten our environment if not properly discarded.

Batteries that end up in landfills and incinerators eventually leak into the environment and end up in the food chain, causing serious health risks to humans and animals. With billions of batteries being purchased in the United States each year, most communities require batteries to be recycled through either public or commercial programs. Find out where to dispose of batteries in your community at this website: http://www.earth911.org.

The Issue:

Paper Waste

The Clean Air Council reports 900 million trees are cut down each year to supply American paper and pulp mills. Paper not only accounts for a waste of trees, but paper waste also accounts for more than 40 percent of the trash going to landfills.

If you think all that paper will just rot quickly, archaeologists from the University of Arizona who studied landfills discovered that it takes a lot longer for paper to decompose than previously thought. These archaeologists discovered newspapers intact and readable from the 1970s.

Landfills all over the country are filling up rapidly and closing at the rate of one per day. Eliminating paper from our waste would nearly double the lives of current landfills, but this takes action by all of us.

So What's Recycling?

Recycling means the item will be broken down and made into something new.

Recycling Paper

Before recycling, waste paper must have all contaminants, such as glass, plastics, paper clips, and staples, removed. The paper is then taken to a paper mill where paper waste is shredded and mixed with water to make a slushy pulp. The pulp is then pumped onto a large moving screen. As the pulp travels down the screen, water is drained and the resulting sheet is pressed between huge rollers which squeeze out most of the water. The semidry web is then run through heated rollers to dry before the finished paper is wound into huge rolls. A slitter cuts the paper into smaller, more manageable rolls, and the paper is ready to print and cut into other paper products.

Use Less Paper and Recycle Paper You Use!

TAKE ACTION

★ Purchase items with less packaging.
★ Bring a reusable bag to the grocery store.
★ Print from your computer only when necessary.
★ Encourage your school to recycle all paper.
★ Use reusable lunch bags, not paper bags.
★ Ask your parents to remove their names from mailing lists.
Go to: The DirectMail.com National Do Not Mail List at https://www.directmail.com/directory/mail_preference/

Make Recycled Paper

What You Need

- 6–8 pages of scrap paper (no tape or staples) torn into small pieces
- 3-gallon (11 L) tub filled with warm water
- Wire clothes hanger
- Knee-high stocking
- Stapler
- Electric blender
- Tiny flower petals or leaves
- Dishtowels

1 Soak paper in water for 4 hours.

2 Pull the hanger into a square. Stretch stocking over hanger and staple to the frame (Fig. 1).

3 Ask a grownup to fill a blender halfway with warm water. Add 2 handfuls of wet paper. Cover blender and blend on medium until mixed.

4 Clean out the large tub and pour in the soupy mixture. Add small petals and leaves. Fill tub with water and mix.

5 Hold the frame flat and dip it into the water mixture. Gently move it back and forth so paper mixture gathers on top. Keep the frame flat and lift it out of the water. Let the water drip (Fig. 2).

6 Flip over screen and onto a dishtowel. Gently press the stocking and push the paper onto the towel as you slowly lift the frame (Fig. 3).

7 Let the paper dry overnight. Make several pieces of paper with the soupy mixture you have. DO NOT wash leftovers down the drain.

Figure 1

Figure 2

Figure 3

Paper or Plastic?

Which is better, paper or plastic grocery bags? It takes 20 to 40 percent less energy to manufacture plastic grocery bags than paper ones. It takes seven trucks to deliver the same number of paper bags as can be carried in one truckload of plastic bags. So which is better? Actually neither. A reusable bag is the best bag to use. Bring reusable bags to the grocery store to carry home your purchases. You'll save precious paper and not have to use plastic bags that aren't biodegradable.

Try This!

Check into disposal options for nonrecyclables, such as printer cartridges, old eyeglasses, paint, cell phones, and other items you should not throw in the garbage. There is a list in the Resources section for many items. Also, check with local organizations. Many, like Girl Scouts, will take some of these recyclables in order to make money for their charity.

GREEN NEWS

According to the Clean Air Council, one ton of paper from recycled pulp saves 17 trees, 3 cubic yards of landfill space, 7,000 gallons of water, 4,200 kilowatt hours (enough to heat your home for half year), 390 gallons of oil, and prevents 60 pounds of air pollutants.

The Issue: Deforestation

About one-fifth of all greenhouse gas emissions in the world can be attributed to deforestation. After the United States and China, Indonesia is the next country to emit the greatest amount of greenhouse gases. That might be hard to believe, since Indonesia is a rural country with few cities, but its rural nature is what is indirectly contributing to emissions. Indonesia emits 3.3 billion tons of carbon dioxide annually, mostly from deforestation. When trees are alive, they absorb carbon dioxide. But when they are burned or cut down through deforestation, they release their stored carbon into the air. In the tropics of Indonesia, living trees not only absorb carbon dioxide, but they also promote cloud formation, which cools the region.

Save Our Trees

★ Use less paper. Print on the back side of previously printed paper, if possible.
★ Help use fewer trees by using recycled paper.
★ Check out the origin of the wood you buy. Make sure it is environ-mentally friendly.
★ Avoid unwanted mail. Call catalog houses and request to have your name removed.
★ Ask a grownup to help you plant a tree.

GREEN NEWS

In 2001 a New Jersey court blocked the town of Asbury Park from repairing its boardwalk because the repairs were to be made with ipe (EE-pay), a rain forest tree. Up to 10,000 trees would be cut down for every 100,000 feet (3 km) of the boardwalk. Instead, the city used recycled rain forest hardwood from dead trees in the rain forest.

Start a New Plant

What You Need

- **An existing houseplant (coleus, ivy, geranium)**
- **Clean scissors**
- **Vase**
- **Water**
- **Plastic bag**
- **Rubber band**

1 Select a stem on the plant with a node, where a leaf is or was attached, and below one or two leaves.

2 Cut the stem right below the node.

3 Place your cutting in a vase of water.

4 Place the plastic bag over the top of the vase and secure it with a rubber band.

5 Check daily for roots. When there is a bunch of roots, transplant your plant to a flowerpot with soil.

GREEN NEWS

Tree experts are working in New York City to find historic trees. Cuttings from these trees will be sent to a scientific tree nursery where they will be reproduced in a plan to add one million trees to the city's streets and parks.

Land **71**

Slash and Burn

In some countries the slash-and-burn method of clearing the forest for agriculture usage is practiced. Slash and burn means the vege-tation is cut down and then burned. This risky, sometimes uncontrollable, method of clearing land not only destroys the trees but also destroys a tremendous amount of a rain forest ecosystem. In addition, the fires pro-duce a large amount of greenhouse gases, including carbon dioxide, methane, ozone, and nitrous oxide.

GREEN NEWS

The native peoples in Pajapan, Mexico, who are skilled carpenters, have been replanting grazing fields with beautiful trees, such as *cocuite* and *granadillo*, which they use to make small carvings for the fair trade market. By cultivating these trees, the community benefits from an economically sustainable industry while protecting their local forests from deforestation.

Support Fair Trade

Buying fair trade can actually change the lives of some of the world's poorest people. Workers earn greater incomes for their labor; and the returns are often invested in community projects, such as health clinics, education, and child care.

Fair trade cooperatives are working to create sustainable good in poor communities. Look for fair trade chocolate and other foods at your local grocery store; you might have to look in the natural food section. Support shops like Ten Thousand Villages that feature fair trade products. Every item you purchase will make a difference in someone's life.

DICTIONARY

So What's Fair Trade?

Fair trade ensures that labor, environmental, and social standards have been followed for the production of goods, like coffee, chocolate, crafts, and clothing.

The Issue:
Aluminum Can Waste

The aluminum beverage can is the most recycled consumer beverage container in the United States. Americans recycle 1,500 aluminum cans every second. But according to the Clean Air Council, Americans still throw away enough aluminum cans to rebuild our commercial air fleet every three months, and enough iron and steel to supply all our nation's automakers every day.

SCIENCE SPEAK

Recycling Aluminum Cans

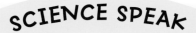

Cans are compacted, shredded, then loaded into melting furnaces. The molten aluminum is poured into ingots, which are then fed into rolling mills that make a long, thin sheet. The metal then goes to can makers who produce can bodies, which are delivered to beverage companies to fill. The filled cans go back on shelves or vending machines. And all this takes place in less than 60 days!

Recycle Aluminum Cans

TAKE ACTION

★ Rinse and squash your cans to keep the volume down.

★ Take your cans to a recyclable collection center every week.

★ Cans are easily recycled to make new cans.

The Issue:
Glass Waste

Using recycled glass uses 40 percent less energy than making glass products from all new materials. Today, almost 22 percent of the glass we produce is recycled. Recycled glass saves energy because crushed glass, called *cullet*, melts at a lower temperature than the raw materials—sand, soda ash, and limestone—used to make glass. Old glass is easily made into new glass jars and bottles or into other glass products like fiberglass insulation. And glass jars and bottles can be recycled over and over again. The glass doesn't wear out. But once glass has been colored, the color cannot be removed, which is why glass must be separated according to color.

Recycle Glass Containers

★ Remove lids or caps and rinse the container.

★ Sort glass containers by color: clear, green, or amber (golden brown).

★ Light bulbs, ceramics, glass mirrors, window-panes, and dishes cannot be recycled.

The Issue:
Plastic Waste

There are more than 10,000 different kinds of plastics. All are made from petroleum products, yet Americans recycle only five percent of all the plastics produced in this country. Recycling recovers the raw material, which can then be used to make new plastic products. Plastics are also incinerated which recovers the chemical energy, which can be used to produce steam and electricity.

Soft-drink bottles made of polyethylene terephthalate (PET) can be melted down and made into carpets, T-shirts, stuffing for ski jackets, or molded into bottles again. Because plastics are made from fossil fuels, think of them as another form of stored energy. Pound for pound, plastics contain as much energy as petroleum or natural gas, and much more energy than other types of garbage. This makes plastic an ideal fuel for waste-to-energy plants that burn garbage and use the energy released during combustion to make steam or electricity.

Recycle Plastics

TAKE ACTION

★ Learn what types of plastics can be recycled by your collector.
★ Follow the wash-and-squash rule: rinse the container and squash it.
★ Throw away the plastic caps.
★ Return your plastic bags to the recycling bins at most grocery stores.

The Issue:
Garbage Waste

We throw away about 43,000 tons of food each day in America. A typical family of four throws away 80 to 150 pounds (36–68 kg) of food a week. If that food were composted and spread back on our gardens and yards, we would require little or no commercial fertilizer.

List of Recyclable Items:
- aluminum cans
- magazines
- water bottles
- junk mail
- food cans
- newspaper
- tissue boxes
- glass bottles and jars
- cardboard cereal boxes
- paper

Recycle School Challenge

Take this challenge to encourage others to recycle. Make a list of recyclable items and bring it to your classroom. Talk to your classmates about the items and how they are recycled. Pick one item from the list and hold a drive at your school. Choose a different item to recycle every two months. Hold a bake sale to pay for the shipping costs if you need funds. Chart your progress during the year. What item were you most successful in recycling? Make a presentation to your school. Have a party at the end of the year to celebrate meeting this terrific challenge.

A Compost Pile

Composting is like baking a cake.
Add the ingredients, stir, "bake," and out comes the compost!

What You Need

- **4 wooden stakes**
- **Hammer**
- **Chicken wire, 8 feet x 2 feet (2.4 m x 61 cm)**
- **Nails**
- **Kitchen scraps ***
- **Straw and water, optional**
- **Shovel**

1 Drive the stakes into the ground. Nail the wire around to make an area about 2 feet (61 cm) square and 2 feet (61 cm) high.

2 Place kitchen or yard wastes into the composting area. Cover kitchen scraps with leaves or grass.

3 The compost pile should be damp to the touch, but not so wet that water comes out when you squeeze it.

4 Add dry straw or sawdust to soggy materials or add water to a pile that is too dry.

* *Note: Do not add meat scraps, bones, dairy products, oil, or fat. They can attract pest animals.*

5 Stir your compost every week by turning it with a shovel. It should be ready to use in one to two months and look like dark, crumbly soil mixed with small pieces of organic material. It will have a sweet, earthy smell.

6 Feed compost to hungry plants by mixing it with the soil.

Create a Compost Pile

★ Set aside a large can or plastic container. Ask your family to place all fruit and vegetable peelings, eggshells, nut shells, and coffee grounds in the container.

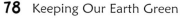

IT Happened in The Past: The Bald Eagle

The bald eagle is an endangered species success story. After World War II, DDT was widely used as a pesticide against malaria-carrying mosquitoes and typhus-carrying lice. It is estimated that 25 million lives were saved because of the use of DDT, but the pesticide was highly toxic to fish.

Birds, like the bald eagle, ate contaminated fish and ingested DDT. The DDT caused the eggshells of the birds to become so brittle and thin that the eggs broke during incubation. This was a major reason that bald eagle populations declined to dangerous levels.

In 1963 scientists counted just over 400 pairs of bald eagles in the lower 48 states. Ten years later, DDT was banned as was the hunting of eagles. Today, there are more than 4,000 pairs of bald eagles in the U.S.

Bald eagle

Rachel Carson

In 1962 the book *Silent Spring*, written by Rachel Carson, was published. Carson wrote about DDT abuse and the destruction of whole ecosystems due to pesticide pollution. *Silent Spring* was credited with sparking the creation of the United States Environmental Protection Agency and the environmental movement. But foremost, *Silent Spring* helped to get the harmful pesticide DDT banned in the United States. With the publication of her book, Rachel Carson showed us the power of words and how one person can make a difference.

DICTIONARY

So What's DDT?

DDT is an insecticide developed to be used against the mosquito that spreads malaria and against the lice that carry typhus. After decades, however, DDT was discovered to have a high toxicity in fish and DDT was banned in the United States in 1973.

....

So What's a Pesticide?

A *pesticide* is a chemical substance used to kill or repel unwanted pests.

....

So What's a Contaminant?

A *contaminant* is a harmful substance that is not naturally present in the environment.

SCIENCE SPEAK

Pesticides

Pests, such as insects, mice, rats, weeds, fungi, bacteria, and viruses, can cause damage to crops or humans; and pesticides destroy these pests. Since pesticides can kill potential disease-causing organisms and control insects, they are sometimes useful; but their use must be strictly controlled. Many household products are pesticides, including insect repellents, mouse poisons, flea and tick sprays and pet collars, kitchen and bath sanitizers, weed killers, and even some swimming pool chemicals.

The Issue:
Chemicals in Farming

Organic farming relies on composting, green manure, and crop rotation instead of synthetic fertilizers to maintain good soil. Pests are not controlled with pesticides but by natural means. In the case of organic meat and milk, antibiotics and growth hormones are prohibited. Although organic foods use "natural" methods, the words natural and organic on food are not the same. Only food labeled "organic" has been certified as meeting USDA organic standards.

In addition to organic food, organic materials are growing in popularity. It takes more than 500 gallons of water to grow enough cotton to make just one t-shirt, and because cotton is prone to boll weevils and other insects, cotton farmers use a great deal of pesticides. Since cotton is naturally a creamy color, in order for cotton to be white, it must be bleached by chemicals that pollute our air and water.

Go Organic

★ Check out the produce section of your local supermarket for certified organic fruits and vegetables.

★ Buy produce in season from local farms practicing organic farming.

★ Look for organic meats, like chicken and beef.

★ Drink organic milk.

★ Ask your student council to find out if your school cafeteria is serving local, organic food. If not, petition for change.

★ Shop for organic cotton products or other "green" fiber clothing.

Make a Difference

You can make a difference by writing your congressional representatives urging them to pass a farm bill that would promote safe alternatives to harmful pesticides like altrazine.

Write a Letter

*Here's how to write a letter to an official about
an issue you'd like them to consider.*

What You Need
- **Paper and pen or computer**
- **Envelope and stamp**

1 Investigate whom you need to send your letter to. (Find out who your U.S. representative is at http://www.congress.org.)

2 Decide whether you want to write or type your letter. Make sure your handwriting is clear and easy to read if you do handwrite it.

3 Ask a grownup to read your letter before you mail it.

4 Address the envelope, include your return address, and place a stamp on the right-hand corner.

Investigate! Evaluate! Evaluate!

DICTIONARY

So What's Altrazine?

Altrazine is a pesticide used by farmers who spray altrazine on their crops to kill bugs and pests that eat the crops.

Your street address
Your city, state, and zip
Date

Dear Senator or Congressman_____,

Pesticides are harmful to our health and yet many farms are still using them to control pests. These harmful chemicals seep into our water supplies and cause damage to our environment.
I ask you to support a Farm Bill that will promote safe alternatives to harmful pesticides, like Altrazine.
Your sincere attention to this matter would be greatly appreciated.

Sincerely,

Your name

STAMP

Your name
Your street address
Your city, state, and zip

Name of Senator or Congressman
His or Her address
His or Her city, state, and zip

The Issue:
Threatened and Endangered Species

A list of threatened animal species, called the Red List, is released each year by the International Union for the Conservation of Nature (IUCN). This list reflects the effects of climate change, habitat destruction, pollution, and over-exploitation of the earth's wildlife. In 2007 the Red List included more than 12,000 species. Over 30 percent of the world's species face the possibility of extinction in the next 50 years. You can take a look at the entire list at http://www.iucnredlist.org/.

Adopt a Wild Animal

TAKE ACTION

★ Give an adopted animal to your friends and family as a birthday gift.

★ Organize a money-raising bake sale to raise money to adopt an animal.

★ Support organizations that help animals, like the Nature Conservancy, the Audubon Society, and the Worldwide Wildlife Fund.

Wild Animal Adoption

There are many agencies through which, for a small donation, you can "adopt" an animal—like whales, orangutans, elephants, and many others. Of course, you don't take the animal home, but the money will help guarantee that these animals do not become extinct.

Adopt an Animal

What You Need

- **Library or computer for research**
- **Markers**
- **Index cards**
- **Poster board**

1 Choose your favorite animal, and research it online or at your school library to find out if your animal falls into one of the Red List endangered categories.

2 Gather facts about your animal and write these on index cards.

3 Using these facts, make a poster to display in your school or home.

4 Invite your friends to adopt animals also. Suggest an "adopt an animal" project for your school class.

Dr. Ian Singleton

EARTH HERO

Since 2001 Dr. Ian Singleton has worked with the Sumatran Orangutan Conservation Program (SOCP) to improve law enforcement against poachers. This has already led to an increase in the amount of illegal pet orangutans being reported and confiscated by authorities. The SOCP also educates the public about the plight of the orangutans, helps with initiatives to protect habitats, and works

to reintroduce former pet orangutans back into the wild. SOCP has taken the lead to monitor orangutans and continue long-term field studies of the species. Dr. Singleton and his program continue to make a difference in the lives of the endangered orangutan.

Red List Highlights

Sumatran Orangutan.
Critically Endangered. The population of this ape has decreased more than 80 percent in the last 75 years due to being hunted for the international pet trade, as well as the destruction of their habitat on the island of Sumatra due to logging. The demand for lumber after the 2004 tsunami has further destroyed their homes.

Mauritius Parakeet.
Down listed from Critically Endangered to Endangered. This parakeet now survives only on the island of Mauritius. Destruction of the bird's habitat caused a severe population decrease, but breeding programs have successfully turned those population numbers around. The bird is still threatened by loss of habitat, but scientists can celebrate some success.

Coachella Valley Fringe-toed Lizard.
Endangered. This lizard makes its home in southern California. Due to agriculture and urban development, the lizard has lost 80 to 90 percent of its habitat.

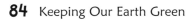

GREEN NEWS

Biologists and engineers are building all sorts of crossings for wildlife, including tunnels, bridges, viaducts, and causeways all over the world.

Banff National Park in Canada has built a bridge for the park's animals. The bridge helps protect black bears, deer, elk, and the rare Canadian lynx. Colorado also plans to create a wildlife bridge over I-70 in Vail. And California biologists are planning a wildlife bridge over I-15 south of Temecula to help wildlife, specifically cougars, travel between the Santa Ana Mountains and the Palomar Mountain.

See if you spot a bridge for animals on your next road trip. Look for a bridge spanning the road planted with trees and other plants. 🍃

Frans Lanting

Not all of the people protecting and conserving our planet are scientists. Everyone can use the talents they have to make a difference. Frans Lanting has been photographing our planet for more than 30 years. He has shown us lionesses in the Okavango Delta, macaws in the Peruvian rain forest, albatross nests on South Georgia Island, and a host of other natural subjects. Together with his wife and partner, Chris Eckstrom, we have been introduced to ecosystems and creatures we might never get to see. How can we protect what we do not know? Frans Lanting's photographs have made a difference. His photographs have put areas on the map for tourists, helped develop ecotourism economies, and also brought attention to many threatened places.

Try This! Take along a field guide on your photography expedition. Learn about the plants and animals you photograph.

Take a Photo

Even plants and animals native to your area might someday be in danger from loss of habitat or pesticides and herbicides. Take photos of them to show your family and friends the beauty we never want to lose.

What You Need
- **A camera**
- **A printer or photo shop**
- **Frames**

1 Focus on a single bird in your backyard for a photo.

2 Focus on a deer, coyote, gopher, or any other wild animal that you see, and shoot its picture.

3 Zoom in close on a native wildflower to study.

4 Shoot a native tree and a close-up of a few of its leaves. A close-up of the tree bark makes an interesting photo.

5 Zoom in on insects such as ants, butterflies, dragonflies, or even spiders and their webs.

6 Blow up your photos, and frame them to share the native wildlife with friends and family.

Kids for Karners

Kids in many different states are working to help save the endangered Karner blue butterfly from going extinct. The postage-size Karner blue butterfly is the state butterfly of New Hampshire. The butterfly is just one of the many endangered species suffering from loss of habitat. In the butterfly's case, habitat goes hand-in-hand with lupine flowers, the only plant Karner blue caterpillars will eat. Wild blue lupines are found in pine barrens and in sandy, dry soils. Kids in the program germinate seeds and plant pine seedlings. They not only help the butterflies, but also help reestablish a native plant population. Kids for Karners are making a difference.

New Hampshire

DICTIONARY

So What's Biodiversity?

Biodiversity is the variety of species in the world or a particular ecosystem.

SCIENCE SPEAK

Biodiversity

So, really, does it matter to us if the Karner blue butterfly or any other species goes extinct? Why is it so important? We don't really know what effect the loss of one species will have on the ecosystem or the planet, but we know if the lupine disappears, so will the Karner blue butterfly. There are many species that rely on other species to live, and one of those species may also hold some importance to our survival. Our world works best with strong biodiversity, meaning there are many different species. It is important to try to protect the earth's diversity of life for each other and for the health of our planet.

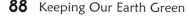

A Recycled Birdfeeder

What You Need

- 1 ½-gallon (2 L) paper milk carton
- Pen
- Ruler
- Scissors
- Nontoxic paints, optional
- 2 small dowels
- Picture-hanging wire
- Birdseed
- Journal

1. Thoroughly wash and rinse milk carton. Allow to dry.

2. With the pen and ruler, draw openings on opposite sides of the carton.

3. Cut along the lines you drew. You may paint the carton with nontoxic paint if you wish.

4. Poke a dowel below each opening on the sides of the carton.

5. Poke a length of wire in the top of the feeder to hang.

5. Add seed to the feeder and hang in a tree that you can see from your window.

6. Keep a journal of the number and species of birds you see every day. Are there different birds in winter and summer?

Energy

"Not only will atomic power be released, but someday we will harness the rise and fall of the tides and imprison the rays of the sun."

—Thomas A. Edison

Video Games, Home Computers, and Cool Cars

As the number of cars, houses, computers, and lights grow throughout the world, more and more energy will be required and used. A day doesn't go by without some mention of energy on our news networks, whether it is the price of gas to fuel our cars, a coal mining accident, or climate change.

Throughout the history of the world's energy, we have made use of fossil fuels: oil, coal, and natural gas. Now we know that coal pollutes our air, and oil and gas will not last forever. We must reduce our energy needs as well as find new sources of energy to meet our requirements.

So What's Greenhouse Gases?

Greenhouse gases are gases—some of which occur naturally and some caused by other factors—which trap heat in the atmosphere and cause global warming.

....

So What's Nonrenewable Energy?

Nonrenewable energy is energy that is generated from sources that cannot be replaced in a short amount of time. These include coal and petroleum products.

....

So What's Renewable Energy?

Renewable energy is energy that is generated from sources that are replenished by nature, like rain and snowfalls. The energy sources are limitless.

SCIENCE SPEAK

Sources of Energy

Renewable energy sources can be replenished (made again) in a short period of time. The five renewable sources used most often are: bio-stored energy, water (hydropower), geo-thermal, wind, and solar.

Nonrenewable energy sources cannot be replenished in a short period of time. Coal, petroleum, natural gas, and propane are all considered fossil fuels because they formed from the buried remains of plants and animals that lived millions of years ago. Uranium ore is not a fossil fuel but is mined and converted to a fuel in nuclear reactors.

Electricity and hydrogen are secondary sources of energy and, thus, different from the other energy sources. We have to use another energy source to make electricity or hydrogen. Secondary sources of energy are used to store, move, and deliver energy in easily usable form.

Explore Electricity

How dependent are you on the electricity in your home? Take the survey below and find out.

What You Need
- **Paper and pencil**

1 Make a chart listing all the rooms in your home.

2 Walk into each room and write down all of the ways electricity is used in that room. How often is it used? How important is each appliance to your family? What can you do without?

3 Write down your findings and share them with your family. Talk about the ways you can conserve electricity in your home.

SCIENCE SPEAK

What Is Electricity?

Electricity is what powers your TV, computer, and furnace. But just what is this power that we cannot see? Electricity began barely 100 years ago, yet now it runs our lives and our world. Electricity is a secondary energy source which means that we get it by converting other sources of energy, like coal, natural gas, oil, or nuclear power—all primary sources of energy. The energy sources we use to make electricity can be renewable or non-renewable, but electricity itself is neither renewable or nonrenewable.

The Issue:
ELectricity Use

In the United States, coal has been and continues to be the source of most electricity, accounting for over half of all electricity generated. Coal is a nonrenewable energy source and the burning of coal adds to greenhouse gases and, thus, to global warming. Although coal is the nation's major fuel for electric power, natural gas is the fastest growing fuel. More than 90 percent of the power plants to be built in the next 20 years will likely be fueled by natural gas.

Reduce Electricity

★ Turn off lights, computer screens, and TVs when not using them.

★ Replace incandescent bulbs with fluorescent bulbs.

★ Ask your parents to turn the thermostat up in the summer and down in the winter.

★ Ask your parents to purchase energy-efficient appliances for your home.

The Issue:
Heating The Home

Over one-half of the homes in the U.S. use natural gas as their heating fuel. Most of the remaining homes use electricity to heat their homes but gas and oil furnaces use electricity to run fans to distribute the heat.

Heating oil is a petroleum product also used by many Americans to heat their homes. Of the 107 million households in the United States, approximately 8.1 million of them use heating oil as the main heating fuel. Residential space heating is the primary use for heating oil, making the demand highly seasonal. Most of the heating oil use occurs during October through March. The area of the country most reliant on heating oil is the Northeast.

SCIENCE SPEAK

Bio-Stored Energy

Ancient plants that processed the sun's energy by photosynthesis are now the oil, coal, and peat we use as fossil fuel. These energy sources are not renewable, and there is a finite supply on our planet.

Reduce Your Heating Needs

TAKE ACTION

★ Wear extra sweaters or sweatshirts in the winter.
★ Wear shorts and short-sleeve shirts in the summer.
★ Check around your windows and doors for leaks in the insulation. Volunteer to help caulk around windows and add insulation to doors.
★ Insulate light switches and electricity outlets on outside walls.

Draft Dodger

Make two draft dodgers that will keep the warm air inside during the winter and the cool air inside during the summer. See how much air you are stopping with the draft dodger by removing it and placing your hand over the bottom of the door. Is there a difference?

WhaT You Need

- **1 pair of old tights**
- **Scissors**
- **Pillow stuffing**
- **Sewing needle**
- **Thread**
- **Fabric Paint**

1 Cut the legs off the pair of tights and stuff each leg with pillow stuffing.

2 Stitch the end of each dodger closed and decorate your dodgers with fabric paint.

3 Place your draft dodgers on the floor in front of a door to keep out cool drafts and use less energy to heat your house.

GREEN NEWS

It would be great if all of those fumes from coal burning could be trapped, wouldn't it? Well, scientists have developed a way to do just that in a process called *carbon sequestration*. This method cuts down on carbon-dioxide emissions.

CoaL USE

About half of the electricity produced in the United States comes from just about the dirtiest fuel around: coal. Coal-fired power plants release carbon-dioxide fumes into the atmosphere, leading to climate change. According to the Sierra Club, 59 percent of America's sulfur-dioxide pollution and 18 percent of the nitrous-oxide pollution is also generated from coal-burning power plants. We have seen that these two compounds are also a major cause of acid rain. Can we move completely away from coal use? The answer is not known, but there are measures being taken to improve the industry.

DICTIONARY

So WhaT's CoaL?

Coal is a combustible black or brownish-black sedimentary rock composed mostly of carbon and hydrocarbons. It is the most abundant fossil fuel produced in the United States.

Heat and Light

Conventional incandescent light bulbs not only emit light, but they also emit heat. A compact fluorescent light bulb emits very little heat. Try this experiment to see the difference.

WhaT You Need

- **White towel**
- **A gooseneck lamp**
- **1 60-watt fluorescent light bulb**
- **Thermometer**
- **Ruler**
- **Pencil and paper**
- **1 60-watt incandescent light bulb**

1 Place the towel on a table and place the lamp on top. Place the fluorescent bulb in the lamp. Place the thermometer on the towel.

2 Measure the distance between the lamp and the thermometer and write down that figure.

3 Shine the light on the thermometer for 10 minutes. Note the temperature and write that down.

4 Turn off the light. Wait for the bulb to cool and the thermometer's temperature to return to room temperature.

5 Replace the bulb with the incandescent bulb.

6 Repeat steps 3 and 4, making sure that the distance from the bulb to the thermometer is the same distance as in the first reading.

7 Note the temperature and write it down.

8 Which bulb was hotter? Which light bulb would you want in your house during a hot summer?

The Issue:
Light Bulbs

Lighting actually accounts for about one-fifth of all the electricity we use in the United States. You can save energy in your house by exchanging incandescent light bulbs for compact fluorescent light bulbs (CFL). They may cost as much as five times that of the incandescents, but they use one-quarter of the electricity and will last several years longer. Over the life of the bulbs, fluorescent light bulbs will actually save money as well as help the environment. These new bulbs contain five milligrams of mercury, so  they will need to be recycled instead of tossing them into your trash. You can find a recycling site near you at http://www.epa.gov/bulbrecycling/.

Try This!

How would you like to prevent 1,000 pounds of carbon-dioxide emissions from being released into the environment? You can. Simply change one light bulb in your house.

DICTIONARY

So What's Photosynthesis?

Photosynthesis is the process by which plants use the energy of the sun to convert water and carbon dioxide to oxygen and carbohydrates.

So What's Electricity?

Electricity is generated at a power plant and runs into your house through wires.

GREEN NEWS

In 2007 the Australian minister of the environment, Malcom Turnbull, announced that Australia will phase out the use of incandescent light bulbs and replace them with fluorescent ones. He claims this will cut 800,000 tons of greenhouse gas emissions by 2012.

Change Your Light Bulbs

★ Exchange every incandescent bulb in the ceiling for a fluorescent bulb.

★ Remove incandescent light bulbs in lamps and replace with fluorescent bulbs.

★ Discuss the possibility of exchanging your outdoor lighting with fluorescent light fixtures.

Energy from Surface Sources

Energy can come from sources that are on the surface of the earth. These include energy from wind, the sun (solar), and hydropower from surface water sources.

Wind Energy

The sun warms the earth, but the earth isn't warmed evenly. It is warmest at the *equator*, the imaginary line that circles the earth, because the equator receives roughly the same amount of sunlight all year. When the air is warmed at the equator, it rises into the atmosphere and flows toward the poles, and the cold air at the poles flows to take the place of the warmer air. This movement creates *wind*. A windmill, or wind turbine, used to generate wind power can harness the wind. It is an inexpensive and clean alter-native power source. A pinwheel is a mini-windmill.

GREEN NEWS

A 1.5 megawatt wind turbine can generate approximately 4.6 million kilowatt hours annually. One turbine could eliminate the need for 383,000 gallons of diesel-fuel generated power. Producing 4.6 million kilowatt hours each year could offset the emissions of 7.1 million pounds of carbon dioxide. That amount of electricity is equivalent to planting 83,000 new trees or driving 75 million fewer miles in an average automobile each year the wind turbine is in operation.

Wind Energy Pinwheel

What You Need

- **8 x 8-inch (20 x 20 cm) sheet of paper**
- **Ruler**
- **Pen or pencil**
- **Scissors**
- **Pin**
- **Pencil with eraser**

1 Lay the sheet of paper on a table.

2 With the ruler, draw a diagonal line from each corner to the opposite corner.

3 With the pencil tip, punch a hole at the point where the two lines intersect, in the middle of the square.

4 Cut along each line until you reach about 1 inch from the center.

5 Poke a small hole with the pin in the left-hand corner of each of the four flaps. No two holes should be next to each other.

6 Hold one of the flaps at the corner with the hole. Curve it over to the center hole. Poke the pin through it to hold in place.

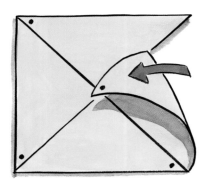

7 Repeat with each flap until the pin is holding all of the flaps.

8 Gently pick up the pinwheel and pin it to the side of the pencil eraser. Turn the pinwheel toward the wind. When the wind hits the center of the pinwheel, it will rotate just like a windmill.

Hydropower

Most of our hydroelectricity is produced through the use of dams. Water behind the dam is released through water wheels called *turbines*, which turn generators that produce electricity. Dams provide much-needed power, water storage, irrigation, and flood control; however, they can also damage our rivers and animals. For instance, on the Columbia River, salmon must swim upstream to their spawning grounds to reproduce, but the series of dams gets in their way. Different approaches to fixing this problem have been used, including the construction of "fish ladders" which help the salmon "step up" the dam to the spawning grounds upstream.

GREEN NEWS

Sometimes dams outlive their usefulness and their ecological costs start to outweigh their benefits. That's when they need to be removed. American Rivers (http://www.americanrivers.org) is one organization helping communities remove harmful, unnecessary dams through their Rivers Unplugged Campaign. Many obsolete dams have already been removed.

BuiLd a Dam

Here's your chance to be an engineer. Try your hand at building and testing your own dam.

WhaT You Need

- **1 ½-gallon (2 L) paper milk carton**
- **8 craft sticks**
- **Scissors**
- **Newspapers**
- **Wood glue**
- **Pottery clay**
- **Assorted sticks, gravel, and dirt**

1 Ask a grownup to cut the top off the milk carton just below the fold and cut off one entire side of the carton.

2 Ask a grownup to cut the craft sticks in half with scissors.

3 Cover your work surface with newspapers. Arrange the craft sticks on the newspapers, laying them side-by-side to form the dam wall. Glue the sticks together and let dry.

4 Place the carton on the table so that the cut-away side is facing up. Start to construct the dam by gluing the wall to the back of the milk carton.

5 Build up your dam by adding a triangle shape of clay over the stick wall you have created. Add sticks, gravel, and dirt over the clay layer. These materials are known as *riprap* in a real dam. You might need to mix more clay with these materials to help them stick to the dam. Press firmly on the dam to make sure all the different layers are tightly attached.

6 Let your dam dry for 1 week.

7 After your dam is thoroughly dry, test the dam. Slowly pour water behind the dam. Does the water seep through or is your dam holding it back?

Solar Power

Solar is the Latin word for sun, and it is a powerful energy source. We use solar power as a source for heat and as a source for energy. The sun powers our planet in many ways, some indirect and others direct. Solar panels, a direct form of energy, energize everything from calculators to houses. Today we can use solar collectors for heating water and air in our homes. If you've seen a house with big shiny panels on the roof, that family is using solar power.

"MY DAD SURE ISN'T SOLAR POWERED."

SCIENCE SPEAK

Photovoltaic Energy

You have probably seen square, flat solar cells on calculators or buildings. These cells, or panels, work to harness the light from the sun and convert it to electricity. The scientific term for this type of solar energy is called *photovoltaic energy*. The cells are known as *photovoltaic cells* (PVs), or solar cells.

Sunlight is made up of particles of solar energy called *photons*. When the photons hit a solar cell, they will be absorbed or reflected or will pass through it depending on the amount of energy they contain. Only the absorbed photons will provide energy to generate electricity.

There are a couple of drawbacks to solar energy. Sunlight is not reliable because not all days are sunny and the area that is required to collect the light to make it worthwhile is very large. Scientists are hard at work developing thin, film solar cells that will be able to absorb an even broader range of light. Watch the news for more on these cells.

Simple Solar Cooker

The next time you go camping or are planning a picnic, you can cook without a campfire with this simple, solar-powered oven.

WhaT You Need
- **Cardboard pizza box**
- **Scissors**
- **Aluminum foil**
- **Glue**
- **Thin sheet of plastic**
- **Black construction paper**

1 With the help of a grownup, cut a flap into the lid of the pizza box. Cut only on three sides, leaving about an inch between the edge of the flap and the edge of the lid. Close the box and pull up the flap.

2 Line the inner side of the flap with aluminum foil to reflect the rays of the sun.

3 Open up the box lid and glue a thin sheet of plastic over the flap opening.

4 Line the inside of the box with aluminum foil and then cover the foil with a layer of black construction paper. Glue the paper in place. The foil reflects the heat of the sun and the black paper will absorb it.

5 Take your finished oven into the sun and try making a melted cheese sandwich or a s'more in your oven. The temperature inside will reach about 200°F (93°C) in the sun. Experiment with other foods.

So What's an Atom?

An *atom* is one of the tiny particles that make up every object in the universe.

....

So What's Radioactive?

Radioactive means that the material is capable of giving off high-energy rays or particles.

Nuclear Energy

Nuclear energy is energy that resides in the nucleus, or core, of an atom. There is enormous energy in the bonds that hold atoms together. Nuclear energy can be used to make electricity, but first the energy must be released. It can be released from atoms in two ways: nuclear fusion and nuclear fission.

Is Nuclear Energy Green?

Nuclear energy has one of the lowest impacts on the environment of any energy source because it emits no pollution, isolates its waste from the environment, and requires a relatively small amount of land.

Nuclear Fission

Fission is the sister to fusion. Instead of two atoms combining to form a new element, fission is the splitting of atoms. Nuclear fission happens when an atom nucleus is split apart and a great deal of energy is released. This reaction is easier to control than fusion, but fission creates radioactive material which, if released, would be very dangerous. This radioactive waste is stored in solid form and within a concrete dome.

Chernobyl, Russia

In 1986 a deadly accident occurred at the nuclear power plant in Chernobyl, Russia. An explosion and fire at the plant led to a release of radioactive material across Russia, Eastern Europe, Scandinavia, and later Western Europe. Thirty-one people died, and thousands were harmed through their contact with the radioactive material. Today, an 18-mile "exclusion zone" remains in which people are not allowed to live. Health problems, however, remain as a result of this disaster.

Nuclear Fusion

Not only does our sun fuel us with solar and wind energy, it also generates its own energy. The sun is a giant ball of gas, composed of about 70 percent hydrogen and about 28 percent helium. These two amounts change over time as the hydrogen atoms combine to form helium atoms in a process called *fusion*. Fusion is like heating two chunks of butter which fuse together and produce more butter. In the case of the sun, this fusion of two compounds also releases energy in the form of light and heat. Fusion is what makes the sun shine and what makes us warm.

Scientists have experimented for years with nuclear fusion, but they have not yet developed a way to harness that energy and sustain it for our use. We know that if they did find a way to sustain it, the energy would be pollution free with no greenhouse gas emissions. Experimentation with nuclear fusion has a long way to go, but it might just end up solving many of our pollution and climate change issues.

IT Happened in The Past: Three Mile Island

1979 MARCH

It is hard to discuss nuclear power plants without mentioning the risk involved in their energy production. If the nuclear plant operates successfully, it is a very clean way to generate electricity; however, accidents have occurred. An accident occurred in Pennsylvania in 1979 at Three Mile Island. One of the nuclear reactors at the plant lost its coolant and overheated. A partial meltdown occurred, and some radioactive waste was released. Although it led to no deaths or injuries to plant workers or members of the nearby community, it brought about sweeping changes involving emergency response planning, reactor operator training, human factors engineering, radiation protection, and many other areas of nuclear power plant operations. It also caused the U.S. Nuclear Regulatory Commission to tighten and heighten its regulatory oversight. Resultant changes in the nuclear power industry and at the NRC had the effect of enhancing safety.

Cooling towers of the Three Mile Island nuclear power plant

Is The Risk Too High?

Nuclear power plants may be the answer to the energy needs in the United States, but there are drawbacks to the plants, and they can divide communities.

WhaT You Need
- **10 friends or classmates**
- **Index cards**

1 Write each of the following "identities" on two cards each:

Nuclear power plant builder
Uranium delivery truck driver
Nuclear power plant manager
Nuclear power plant inspector
Home owner with family

2 Divide your friends or class into two groups. One group will be for building the nuclear plant. The other group will be against the plant.

3 Divide the index cards among 10 friends, giving five to one group and five to the other.

4 Have a community meeting with one identity from each group debating the same identity from the other group. One group must discuss the benefits of nuclear energy and its safety, specifically as it relates to the "identity." The other identities must argue against building the power plant. For instance, one plant manager must give the dangers of running the plant while the other manager gives the benefits of running the plant.

5 After the meeting, discuss which group made a better case.

Biofuels

Biofuels may be the answer to our country's fuel independence. Corn, soybean, grass, used cooking oil, and other materials can be turned into ethanol, a fuel that could prevent millions of tons of carbon emissions from entering our air. As promising as biofuel production is, however, it also has its drawbacks. There are some 114 ethanol plants in the United States, many of which are using fossil fuels of natural gas and even coal to run the processors. But because ethanol can corrode gas pipelines, the ethanol must be trucked to consumer points, again using fossil fuel. So with any energy issue, there is no free lunch.

DICTIONARY

So What's a Biofuel?

Biofuels are nonpetroleum fuel alternatives made from plant matter and animal wastes, such as alcohol made from fermented sugar or corn.

Termite Enzymes

The process by which ethanol is produced from grass requires enzymes to break down the plant's cellulose. Those enzymes that may prove to work the best might end up being found in the stomach of a South American rain forest termite. Scientists are continually searching for just the right enzyme.

The Issue: Biofuels

Biofuel may be a terrific fuel alternative, but as the saying goes, "there's no free lunch." Ethanol, a fuel made from corn, increases the demand for corn crops that are used as feed, sweeteners, and the manufacture of other products. Consumers might see an increase, then, in the price of chicken, beef, eggs, milk, cereal, and soda. There might even be a price increase in such things as toothpaste, soap, and diapers that use corn in their manufacturing. In addition, the corn crops might compete with other fruit and vegetable crops and a rise in their prices might follow.

Thousands of people marched on Mexico City in January 2007 to protest the high cost of corn tortillas, which was linked to the demand for ethanol.

Work for Cleaner School Buses

TAKE ACTION

★ See if your school buses turn off their engines instead of idling.

★ Find out if older school buses have been replaced with more energy efficient ones.

★ Research biodiesel fuel.

★ See if your school buses can run on biodiesel.

★ Find out if biodiesel fuel is available where you live.

Ocean Thermal Energy

All that water covering the surface of the earth acts like a solar collector to gather heat from the sun's rays. By using the sun's rays, energy can be generated in three different ways. We call these ways *open-cycle*, *closed-cycle*, and *hybrid-cycle*, which is a combination of the open and closed.

Ocean Energy

The earth's oceans cover almost three-quarters of our planet and have the potential to provide two kinds of energy. The first is called *thermal energy*, which comes from the heat of the sun; and the second is *mechanical energy*, which comes from the motion of the waves and tides. Because there are few ocean power plants, we have not been able to generate much energy from the ocean, but there is the potential to generate enough renewable energy to power our homes and businesses.

Tides and Waves

Tides and waves are intermittent energy sources because they are not constant, but they can still be useful for energy. A dam or *barrage* is used to force tidal water into and out of reservoirs just like in a hydroelectric plant. This process works best in areas where the tides have at least a 16-foot (4.9 m) increase. There is an ocean power plant in France that generates enough ocean energy to power 240,000 homes.

Wave energy is smaller and is generally used to power a light on a buoy or a tiny lighthouse. The waves drive hydraulic pumps or can be used to compress air within a container. In each case, energy results from a generator being activated.

So What's Geothermal Energy?

The word geothermal comes from the Greek words *geo* (earth) and *therme* (heat). So, geothermal energy is heat from within the earth. We can use the steam and hot water produced inside the earth to heat buildings or generate electricity. *Geothermal energy* is a renewable energy source because the water is replenished by rainfall and the heat is continuously produced inside the earth.

SCIENCE SPEAK

Geothermal Electricity

The direct use of hot water as an energy source has been around since ancient times. The Romans, Chinese, and Native Americans used hot mineral springs for bathing, cooking, and heating. Today, many hot springs are still used for bathing, and many people believe the hot, mineral-rich waters have natural healing powers.

After bathing for medicinal purposes, the most common direct use of geothermal energy is for heating buildings. Hot water near the earth's surface can be piped directly into buildings and industries for heat.

Geothermal power plants use hydrothermal resources which have two common ingredients: water (hydro) and heat (thermal). Geothermal plants require high-temperature (300°–700°F or 149°–371°C) hydrothermal resources that may come from either dry-steam wells or hot-water wells. We can use these resources by drilling wells one to two miles (1.6–3.2 km) deep into the earth and piping the steam or hot water to the surface.

The United States generates more geothermal electricity than any other country, but the amount of electricity it produces is less than 1 percent of the electricity required. To date, only four states have geothermal plants: California, Nevada, Hawaii, and Utah.

Steam Energy

Geothermal energy works similarly to the steam that is released from boiling water on the stove. See how much energy is released by steam in this experiment.

What You Need

- **Saucepan**
- **Water**
- **Aluminum foil**
- **Pencil**
- **Potholder**
- **Pinwheel**

1 Fill the saucepan with water. Tightly cover the pan with foil.

2 With the pencil, poke a hole in the center of the aluminum foil.

3 Ask a grownup to help with the rest of the experiment. Place the pot on the stove and heat. When the water boils, steam will rise out of the hole in the foil.

4 Use the potholder to remove the pot from the heat.

5 Hold the pinwheel over the hole into the steam. Does your pinwheel turn? How fast does it turn? Imagine steam rising out of the earth. In a geothermal plant, the steam is used to move a turbine, similar to how the wind moves a wind turbine. The turbine activates a generator to produce electricity.

Geothermal Energy

The earth's core, 4,000 miles (6,437 km) deep, can reach a temperature of 9,000°F (5,000°C). That heat flows from the core outward. Sometimes we see the direct result of that heat when volcanoes erupt. More often the hot magma, or molten rock, stays underneath the surface of the earth and warms rocks and water below the surface. Sometimes the water rises to the surface as hot springs and geysers, like Old Faithful, but much of it stays underground.

GREEN NEWS

China has been burning coal to generate energy for many years. The result is polluted air and very polluted cities. In contrast, Iceland's capital city, Reykjavik, has crystal clean air due to the fact that the city gets 100 percent of its heat and 40 percent of its electricity from geothermal power. Hydropower furnishes the rest of the electricity produced. This tiny country has roughly 130 volcanoes that bring magma close to the surface. Steam is formed when the magma comes in contact with groundwater. The steam is tapped to generate clean electricity. Engineers from Iceland traveled to China to help the Chinese generate geothermal power. Plans are to use the geothermal power in some of the 2008 Olympic venues. 🍃

The Issue:
Packaging

It takes fossil fuel to make the packaging we use, including plastic wrap, paper, and plastic containers. Today, things we buy are not just packaged in one package; but often, food items, toys, and electronics are packaged and then that package is repackaged. Think about the CDs and DVDs you buy. How many plastic packages do these have? Look at the toy aisle at the store. How many double packages do you see there? All of this packaging wastes fuel.

Try To Save Energy

TAKE ACTION

★ Think about what you buy when you go shopping. Shop for items that use less packaging.

★ Encourage grownups to buy cars that are fuel-efficient. Use public transportation, bicycles, or walk instead of driving whenever possible to do so safely.

★ Buy less plastic. Substitute glass containers that are reusable for disposable plastic containers.

★ Purchase clothing made from natural fabrics instead of synthetic fabrics. Use reusable containers to store your leftovers.

GREEN NEWS

Your fleece jacket, made from Polartec, Capilene, or Patagonia fleece, can be recycled into new fabric by Patagonia outdoor gear company. Patagonia began the Common Threads Garment Recycling program in 2005. The old garments are melted down and new polyester fabric is produced. The recycling process, which requires less oil to create the new fabric, can reduce greenhouse gas emissions by 71 percent. Check out Patagonia online (http://www.patagonia.com/recycle) for more information. 🍃

Electric Cars

Electric cars have come and gone and are back again. This time they might just be back for good. We know gasoline-powered cars pollute and keep us dependent on foreign oil. Electric cars offer us cars without greenhouse-gas emitting tailpipes. They also release us from our dependence on foreign oil, but that has to do with pure electric cars, not hybrids. Hybrid cars still use gasoline but rely predominantly on an electric charge. The gasoline is needed when the car needs more power, but the electric charge allows them to get much better gas mileage.

There's No Free Lunch

Electric cars are great, but where is the battery energy coming from? The downside is power plants are needed to charge those batteries.

Dr. Angela Belcher

EARTH HERO

A materials chemist at Massachusetts Institute of Technology (MIT), Dr. Angela Belcher is working to change how we think about a lot of things, including batteries. The batteries we use today are difficult to dispose of and generate a lot of waste during their production. Dr. Belcher's project is not building a better battery, but growing a better battery. She is working with an engineered virus called M13 bacteriophage. The virus coats itself with inorganic materials, such as gold and cobalt oxide, then forms a long, tubular strand similar to a wire, which is a fundamental component of a battery. Imagine having a living virus powering your car or computer. No wonder Dr. Belcher was named 2006 Research Leader of the Year and a member of "*Scientific American 50*" by *Scientific American* magazine.

Make a Simple Battery

What You Need
- **Grownup**
- **Knife**
- **1 lemon**
- **1 copper penny**
- **1 galvanized (zinc coated) nail**
- **Volt meter**

1 Have a grownup cut a slit in the side of the lemon, big enough to hold the penny. Insert the penny into the slit.

2 Push the nail into the other side of the lemon making sure it DOES NOT touch the penny. The nail and the penny have now become the electrodes of your lemon battery. The acidic lemon juice is the electrolyte that will conduct the electric current.

3 Have a grownup connect a volt meter to the electrodes to measure the voltage of your lemon battery.

GREEN NEWS

We've seen many types of alternative energy. The hydrogen fuel cell is another source that is now beginning to power some buses and may one day power our cars. These cells act a bit like a battery; but unlike a battery which stores energy, hydrogen fuel cells need to be fed hydrogen to stay powered. The only thing these vehicles discharge is water. There are cars and buses already designed and being sold that will run on these fuel cells, but fueling stations are currently very limited. Even so, since 1999 California has put nine of these buses on the roads. They are clean, quiet, and have zero emissions. As more fueling stations become available, cars running on hydrogen fuel cells can be sold in more states than just California. These cells may be able to provide a clean-fuel alternative to gasoline-powered engines.

Earth Day

Earth Day is a wonderful day to celebrate our planet, plan a community cleanup, or take on one more green activity; but we must remember that our planet doesn't need us just one day each year. We all must work every day throughout the year to make a difference.

It's easy. Making the choice to recycle that drink bottle you had for lunch or changing that light bulb in your room does make a difference. Just think how much cleaner our world would be if everyone did just one thing—or even two or three.

Gaylord Nelson

EARTH HERO

In 1963, Senator Gaylord Nelson had an idea to ask President John F. Kennedy to tour the nation in order to focus attention on environ-mental issues. Although President Kennedy's conservation tour was not successful, Senator Nelson did not give up on the ecological issues. He continued to speak out about the environment. Six years later, Nelson developed the idea for Earth Day. The first Earth Day was held on April 22, 1970. An estimated 20 million people from thousands of schools and communities participated. Although Senator Nelson passed away in 2005, his legacy continues.

President Bill Clinton awarded Gaylord Nelson the Presidential Medal of Freedom in 1995 saying, "as the founder of Earth Day, he is the grandfather of all that grew out of that event. He also set the standard for people in public service to care about the environment and try to do something about it."

Be a Green Family

Is your family green? Take this quiz and find out!
Give yourself 10 points for each yes answer.

1 Did someone in your family walk, ride a bike, or ride public transportation this week?

2 Did your family recycle paper this week?

3 Did your family recycle anything in addition to paper this week, like aluminum cans, glass bottles, or plastic containers?

4 Did you look for food grown within 30 miles from home?

5 Did you support any environmental cause in the past year with time or money?

6 Have you changed any incandescent light bulbs to compact florescent light bulbs?

7 Does your family compost or mulch your grass clippings and lawn debris?

8 Do you have a family vegetable garden?

9 Do you turn off your lights, TV, and computer monitor when you leave a room?

10 Have you visited a wildlife sanctuary, national park, or natural place this year?

Add up your score. If you scored 90 points or above, your family is green! Keep going and inspire others!

If you scored 60–80 points, you are green friendly and doing fine! See if you can add anything to your goals.

If you scored 50 or below, your family could do more. Make a plan and help your family go green!

Resources

Organizations

Children of the Earth United
P.O. Box 816
Columbia, MD 21044
(443) 321-4617
http://www.childrenoftheearth.org/
Children of the Earth United is a great online place to
share your thoughts and pictures about our earth. It's also
a great place to read poems and stories from kids around
the world.

Coalition for Sonoran Desert Protection
300 E. University, #120
Tucson, AZ 85705
(520) 388-9925
http://www.sonorandesert.org
Over 40 conservation and community groups formed the
Coalition for Sonoran Desert Protection in 1998 after the
pygmy-owl was placed on the endangered species list.
Today the Coalition is working to establish the strongest
species and habitat protections possible under the Sonoran
Desert Conservation Plan (SDCP).

Desert Watch
Northern Jaguar Project
2114 West Grant Road, # 121
Tucson, AZ 85745
(520) 623-9653 ext. 5
http://www.desertwatch.org
Desert Watch is an independent, nonprofit organization
based in Tucson, Arizona. It is a partnership between
scientists, private landowners, indigenous peoples,
grassroots and national conservation organizations,
resource managers, and government agencies dedicated to
protecting jaguars and to developing an arid lands
conservation strategy for North America.

Environmental Protection Agency (EPA) Kids Club
http://www.epa.gov/kids/
Explore the environment and learn how to protect it
through fun games and activities. Sign up and you'll get a
membership certificate and access to even more activities.
Complete environmental projects and earn stickers to add
to your membership certificate.

Greenpeace USA
702 H Street, NW
Washington, D.C. 20001
(202) 462-1177
http://www.greenpeace.org/usa/
Greenpeace's philosophy is "ordinary people can

accomplish extraordinary things." Founded by a group of
ordinary citizens in 1971, Greenpeace has worked tirelessly
on behalf of the environment on so many issues. Check out
the web site for information of many different
environmental programs and Greenpeace's initiatives.

Kid's Ecology Corps
1350 East Sunrise Blvd.
Fort Lauderdale, FL 33304
(954) 524-0366
http://www.kidsecologycorps.org/
Inspiring kids to make environmental action a part of their
everyday lives.

Kids F.A.C.E.
P.O. Box 158254
Nashville, TN 37215
(615) 331-7381
http://www.kidsface.org
Founded by a kid for kids, this organization's mission is to
provide information about issues to children, facilitate youth
involvement, and to recognize those accomplishments.
Check out the web site, and form your own chapter.

National Audubon Society
700 Broadway
New York, NY 10003
(212) 979-3000
http://www.audubon.org
The National Audubon Society has worked for decades to
conserve and restore our natural ecosystems. Classroom
kits for grades 3–6 are available through Audubon
Adventures, and middle school students can take part in
Audubon Adventures After School.

National Wildlife Federation
11100 Wildlife Center Drive
Reston, VA 20190
(800) 822-9919
http://www.nwf.org
A large, member-supported conservation group designed to
educate, inspire, and assist individuals and organizations of
diverse cultures to protect the environment and preserve
wildlife.

The Nature Conservancy
4245 North Fairfax Drive, Suite 100
Arlington, VA 22203-1606
(703) 841-5300
http://www.nature.org
The Nature Conservancy's mission is to preserve the plants,
animals, and natural communities that represent the

diversity of life on earth by protecting the lands and waters they need to survive. The conservancy has already protected over 116 million acres worldwide, including numerous projects in North and South America, Asia, the Caribbean, and Central America.

Rainforest Action Network
221 Pine Street, 5th floor
San Francisco, CA 94104
(415) 398-4404
http://www.ran.org/ran/
Check out the organization's kid page at
http://rainforestheroes.com
There are also great resources for teachers.

Rainforest Alliance
665 Broadway, Suite 500
New York, NY 10012
(212) 677-1900
http://www.rain forest-alliance.org/
Promoting biodiversity and working to provide sustainable livelihoods in the world's rain forests. Kids can check out the Rainforest Alliance's coloring pages and other activities.

Rainforest Foundation U.S.
32 Broadway, Suite 1614
New York, NY 10004
(212) 431-9098
http://www.rainforestfoundation.org
The Rainforest Foundation is working to protect over 75,000 square miles of rainforest in partnership with the region's native populations.

Sierra Club
85 Second Street, 2nd Floor
San Francisco, CA 94105
(415) 977-5500
http://www.sierraclub.org
"Explore, enjoy and protect the planet." With that motto, it's no wonder the Sierra Club has been in existence for over 100 years. Check out the Club's programs for kids at the Building Bridges site: http://www.sierraclub.org/youth

Tropical Rainforest Coalition
21730 Stevens Creek Blvd., Suite 102
Cupertino, CA 95014
http://www.rainforest.org/
"Saving rainforests for Earth's children, for Earth's future." Tropical Rainforest Coalition also sponsors the Save-an-Acre and Save-a-Species programs. For a donation of $50, the profit from one bake sale, you can save one acre of rainforest through the coalition's program.

Places to Visit

Arizona-Sonora Desert Museum
2021 North Kinney Road
Tucson, AZ 85743
http://www.desertmuseum.org
This is a great place to start exploring the American desert. You'll see tons of wildlife and can particiapte in many different programs.

EcoTarium
222 Harrington Way
Worcester, MA 01604
(508) 929-2700
http://www.ecotarium.org
This museum of science and nature has some great exhibits to explore including Water Planet, focusing on the role of water, and Thinking Globally, Abiding Locally, focusing on energy uses.

United States National Parks
http://www.nps.gov
There are spectacular national parks all across America that sponsor Junior Ranger programs for you to participate in. All of the parks are unique and offer different programs and activities for families. Visit the website to find a park nearby or to plan your next family vacation. Take part in the National Parks Passport program, and collect stamps at all the parks you visit!

On the Issues

Global Warming
• Check out the Sierra Club's It Takes 2 campaign to fight global warming at http://www.sierraclub.org/twopercent/
• Recycle your old fleece at http://www.patagonia.com/recycle
• Forecast Earth at the Weather Channel http://climate.weather.com

Secondhand Smoke and Tobacco Use
• Tobacco Free Kids http://www.tobaccofreekids.org/
• Stop Targeting Kids http://www.stoptargetingkids.com/
• The Foundation for a Smoke-Free America http://www.notobacco.org/
• Get Real Colorado http://www.getrealcolorado.com/
• Get Outraged Massachusetts http://www.getoutraged.com/
• New Jersey Teens Are Not For Sale http://www.njnotforsale.com/rebel/
• Stand On The Line — Ohio http://www.standonline.org/
• Oklahoma SWAT http://www.okswat.com/

Waste/Recycle

Toothbrushes can be recycled into plastic lumber and yogurt cups at Recycline http://www.recycline.com. Sneakers can be used to make sports surfaces at Nike's ReUse A Shoe http://www.nikereuseashoe.com. Give your near-new running sneakers to One World Running, and they'll find a new home with someone in Africa or another part of the world, http://oneworldrunning.blogspot.com/.

Send your old cell phone to Collective Good, and they'll refurbish it and make it affordable to someone in a developing country http://www.collectivegood.com.

According to Recycle Place, it takes more than three quarts of oil to produce one laser cartridge, so recycle it! Recycle Place not only will recycle it for you, they will send you a dollar for each cartridge you send them. Learn more at http://www.recycleplace.com/.

Green Businesses

A "green" business is socially and environmentally responsible. It may mean that the business promotes fair trade or recycling, or developed a more eco-friendly product. Co-Op America has a national directory of green businesses. These businesses are carefully screened before they can become members of this list. Here's how you can learn more about them and support them: http://www.coopamerica.org/pubs/greenpages/

Wind Energy

Explore National Geographic's interactive web page on wind energy. You can even engineer your own wind turbine. http://green.nationalgeographic.com/environment/global-warming/wind-power-interactive.html

Adoption Programs

Adopt An Acre. Become a Rainforest Ranger and help save the rainforest through The Center for Ecosystem Survival. http://www.savenature.org/adoptacre.html

Adopt A Manatee. Save the Manatee Club offers manatees for adoption. You will receive a photo of your manatee and a biography so that you can learn more about the manatee you are supporting. Your support helps fund manatee rescue, rehabilitation and research. http://www.savethemanatee.org/

Adopt A Reef. Help protect the ocean by adopting a coral reef through The Center for Ecosystem Survival. http://www.savenature.org/adoptreef.html

Adopt a Stream. Many organizations have adopt-a-stream programs, including Georgia's Environmental Protection Division, Massachusetts Department of Fish and Game, Virginia's Department of Conservation and Recreation, and Clinton River Watershed Council. Participants in the programs help monitor and protect their local streams.

Adopt a Watershed. Find out what you can do to protect your local watershed through the Environmental Protection Agency's Adopt a Watershed Campaign. http://www.epa.gov/adopt/

Pollution

The Blacksmith Institute (http://www.blacksmithorganization.org) releases a list each year of the ten most polluted places on the planet. They take all sorts of things into account, such as the severity or seriousness of the poison or toxin causing the pollution, the path the toxin has taken, and how many people might be affected. In 2007 the Institute came up with a list of areas, some remote, some with pollution possibly affecting millions. India, China, and Russia lead the list, each with two sites. Peru, Zambia, Ukraine, and Azerbaijan each have one site. Although the pollution varied, much of it was a result of mining activities. Research each of these sites, and find out if and how they are being cleaned and restored.

Places for 2007
1. Sumgayit, Azerbaijan: 275,000 people possibly affected
2. Linfen, China: 3 million people possibly affected
3. Tianying, China: 140,000 people possibly affected
4. Sukinda, India: 2.6 million people possibly affected
5. Vapi, India: 71,000 people possibly affected
6. La Oroya, Peru: 35,000 people possibly affected
7. Dzerzhinsk, Russia: 300,000 people possibly affected
8. Norilsk, Russia: 134,000 people possibly affected
9. Chernobyl, Ukraine: possibly 5.5 million people affected
10. Kabwe, Zambia: 255,000 people possibly affected

Green Camps for Kids

Northeastern U.S.
Audubon Summer Camp
Sharon, CT
http://www.audubon.org/local/sanctuary/sharon/education/camp.html
Week-long camps during the summer for kids

Flying Deer Nature Center
New Lebanon, NY
http://flyingdeernaturecenter.org/
"Fostering respect for the Earth, for each other, and for ourselves."
Summer programs available

Four Feathers Wilderness Programs
Westchester County, NY
http://www.fourfeatherswildernessprograms.com/programs.html
Camp programs, mentoring programs, and workshops available

White Pine Programs
Cape Neddick, ME
http://www.whitepineprograms.org/article/view/1828/
Summer camp, Outdoor Girls program, Young Naturalists program, and Homeschoolers program

Southeastern U.S.
Camp Explore: The University of Tennessee
Greeneville, TN
http://clydeaustin4hcenter.com/4hcamp.htm
Summer camp offering hands-on environmental education activities

School House of Wonder
Durham, NC
http://www.schoolhouseofwonder.org/
Nature School, Outdoor School, and many other programs

Southwestern U.S.
Arizona-Sonora Desert Museum
Tucson, AZ 85743
http://www.desertmuseum.org/kids/camp_page.php
The museum runs a terrific summer camp, called Earth Camp, in partnership with the University of Arizona College of Science. There is also a Museum Explorers Camp for you to check out.

Midwestern U.S.
Owl Creek Programs
Bloomington, IN
http://www.owlcreekprograms.com/index.html
Naturalist studies and other outdoor programs

Western U.S.
Audubon Starr Ranch Sanctuary
Trabuco Canyon, CA
http://www.starrranch.org/education.htm
Check out the Sanctuary's Ecology and Junior Biologist programs.

Wilderness Youth Project
Santa Barbara, CA
http://www.wyp.org/programs/kids.htm
After school and summer programs for kids

For More Information from the Author

http://www.nancycastaldo.com

Index